Rainbow Edition

Reading Mastery VI
Teacher's Guide

Siegfried Engelmann • Jean Osborn • Steve Osborn • Leslie Zoref

Macmillan/McGraw-Hill
Columbus, Ohio

The authors gratefully acknowledge the students and teachers who used preliminary versions of *Reading Mastery VI*. Special thanks to the following teachers: Sandra Boileau, Margaret Dyson, Vickie Huls, Kaye LeFrancq, Brenda Searby, William Sipple, and Mary Wright.

We also thank Susan Hanner, Larry Jarchow, Joan Podgorski, Carl Strasser, and Suzanne Sumner for their help in preparing the manuscript. We particularly thank Dorothy Collins for her consistently fine editing and expert advice.

SRA Macmillan/McGraw-Hill
250 Old Wilson Bridge Road
Suite 310
Worthington, Ohio 43085
Printed in the United States of America.
ISBN 0-02-686410-X
1 2 3 4 5 6 7 8 9 0 IPC 99 98 97 96 95 94

Contents

Objectives

Reading Mastery VI teaches students to read for purpose and understanding. Students in the program

- read a wide variety of narrative and expository prose
- answer comprehension questions about the reading selections
- work comprehension, reference and study skill exercises
- apply information from factual articles and comprehension passages
- decode accurately and quickly
- learn the meanings of vocabulary words that occur in the stories
- compare story characters, settings, plots and themes
- complete daily writing assignments

Reading a wide variety of narrative and expository prose

Reading Mastery VI prepares students for the challenges of reading at the adult level. The program features both classic and modern literature, as well as a broad range of expository prose. The students read complete novels, short stories, poems, biographies, factual articles, comprehension passages, and a play. Novels and longer stories are divided into parts and presented over a span of lessons.

Answering comprehension questions about the readings

The teacher material contains specific comprehension questions that the teacher asks both during and after the daily readings. The students answer these questions orally. The student material contains written comprehension questions. The students write the answers to these questions independently. All of the comprehension questions are based on the readings, and they teach a number of important comprehension skills, such as understanding perspectives, identifying motives, developing vocabulary and interpreting themes.

Working comprehension, reference and study skill exercises

In addition to answering questions about the stories, the students work a variety of skill exercises that appear in the student material. These exercises teach a wide range of skills, including outlining, making inferences, identifying contradictions, interpreting figurative language, following directions, interpreting maps and graphs, and analyzing arguments. The skill exercises are a significant part of every lesson.

Applying information from factual articles and comprehension passages

Stories and novels that contain a great deal of new information are preceded by comprehension passages or factual articles. These passages and articles present background information that helps the students to comprehend the stories and novels more fully. The passages and articles also prepare the students for the kinds of expository prose found in social studies and science textbooks.

Decoding accurately and quickly

Accurate decoding is a prerequisite for good comprehension, and oral reading is an effective procedure for improving decoding skills. The students read both orally and silently in every lesson. At the beginning of each lesson, the students read lists of new words that will occur in the story for that lesson. The students read these lists in unison. On some lessons, the students take turns reading the story aloud, while staying within a specified decoding error limit.

Learning the meanings of vocabulary words that occur in the stories

Vocabulary instruction is a part of every lesson. During this instruction, the students learn the meanings of vocabulary words and phrases that will appear in the stories. The students practice using the vocabulary words before reading the stories. After the students read the stories, they complete written vocabulary exercises and, in some lessons, crossword puzzles. The stories and exercises provide a continuous review of all vocabulary words taught in the program.

Comparing story characters, settings, plots and themes

Many of the comprehension questions require the students to compare story elements. For example, the students compare the traits of different characters and predict how different characters would act in a variety of situations. The students compare settings by using maps and lists of details. They also compare plots and narrative events, as well as themes and morals. The program's emphasis on comparison helps build the students' organizational and analytical skills.

Completing writing assignments

In every lesson, the students write a brief paragraph on a given topic. Many of the topics require the students to make judgments about the stories. The students are asked to explain their judgments by giving specific evidence from the stories. Other topics encourage the students to interpret stories according to their own experiences and to relate story events to their own lives. The assignments also build writing and reasoning skills. In some lessons, the students write stories and poems of their own.

The Program

Reading Mastery VI contains 120 lessons. A complete lesson plan is provided for each lesson. The lessons consist of teacher-directed activities and activities the students work on independently. Some lessons also contain special projects and optional discussion questions. Finally, as an optional supplementary activity, there are study guides for five novels, to be presented after the students complete lesson 120.

Reading Mastery VI is designed for students who read at about a 6.0 grade level as measured by a standardized achievement test. *Reading Mastery VI* can be used with students who have completed *Reading Mastery V* or any other fifth grade reading program. A placement test (see page 42) may also be used to determine whether students can be appropriately placed in *Reading Mastery VI.*

Materials

The program consists of two *Presentation Books* for the teacher, a student *Skillbook*, a student *Workbook* and a student *Textbook.*

The *Presentation Books* contain

- 120 lessons that provide specific instructions for presenting every activity in each day's lesson
- reproductions of *Textbook* pages
- reproductions of *Workbook* pages with answer keys
- answer keys for *Skillbook* exercises
- a glossary of vocabulary words

The *Skillbook* contains

- vocabulary word lists
- story items
- skill items
- review items
- writing assignments
- special projects

The *Skillbook* is non-consumable. The students write answers for *Skillbook* items on lined paper.

The *Workbook* contains

- story items
- skill items
- review items
- crossword puzzles

The *Workbook* is consumable. *Workbook* exercises are completed in the *Workbook.*

The *Textbook* contains

- novels
- short stories
- poems
- biographies
- a play
- comprehension passages
- factual articles
- a glossary of vocabulary words

The *Textbook* contents are listed below.

Lessons	**Story/Author/Description**
1	**Life in the 1930's** - A comprehension passage that provides background information for the story *The Doughnuts.*
1 – 3	**The Doughnuts** - Robert McCloskey - A humorous story about an automatic doughnut machine.
4	**Two Old Stories** - A factual article about *The Illiad* and *The Odyssey.*
5 – 13	**The Odyssey** - Homer - A prose translation of the epic poem about the adventures of Odysseus.
14 – 20	**The Spider, the Cave and the Pottery Bowl** - Eleanor Clymer - A modern story about an Indian girl who lives on a mesa.
21 – 22	**Sailing in the 1890's** and **Steamers** - Comprehension passages about ships and sailing.
21 – 23	**The Voyage of the Northern Light** - J.T. Trowbridge - An adventure story that takes place near Nova Scotia.
24	**Ireland** - A comprehension passage about Irish immigrants.
24 – 26	**Mrs. Dunn's Lovely, Lovely Farm** - Myron Levoy - A humorous story about Irish immigrants living in New York City.

27 **O. Henry and New York** - A comprehension passage about O. Henry and New York.

27 – 28 **The Last Leaf** - O. Henry - A poignant story about three artists living in Greenwich Village.

29 **Demeter and Hades** - A comprehension passage about a Greek goddess and a Greek god.

29 – 34 **Persephone** - Nathaniel Hawthorne - The Greek myth about Persephone's adventures in the underworld.

33 **Pomegranates** - A comprehension passage about pomegranates.

35 **The Tide Rises, the Tide Falls** - Henry Longfellow- A poem about people and the sea.

36 **Introduction to Sara Crewe** - A comprehension passage about the novel *Sara Crewe*.

37 – 49 **Sara Crewe**- Frances Hodgson Burnett - A romantic novel about the experiences of a girl living in a boarding school in London.

39 **The Bastille** - A comprehension passage about the Bastille.

50 **Guy de Maupassant** - A biographical sketch of the author of *The Necklace.*

50 – 51 **The Necklace** - Guy de Maupassant - The classic story about a lost necklace.

52 – 54 **Mystery Yarn** - Robert McCloskey - A humorous story about a string-saving contest.

55 – 57 **A White Heron** - Sarah Orne Jewett - A realistic story about a girl's love for a heron.

58 **Written in March** - William Wordsworth - A poem about the coming of spring.

59 – 60 **San Francisco Bay** and **More About San Francisco Bay** - Comprehension passages about San Francisco Bay.

59 – 70 **The Cruise of the Dazzler** - Jack London - A novel about pirates in San Francisco Bay.

61 **Tillers** - A comprehension passage about tillers.

71 **A Game in Mudville** - A comprehension passage about baseball.

71 – 72 **Casey at the Bat** - Ernest Thayer - The classic poem about mighty Casey's strike-out.

73 **The Solar System** - A comprehension passage about the solar system.

73 – 75 **The Star** - H.G. Wells - A science fiction story about a star that enters the solar system.

76 **The Civil War** - A comprehension passage about the Civil War.

76 – 82 **Harriet Tubman** - Talbot Bielefeldt - A biography of the famous Underground Railroad conductor.

83 – 85 **All in Favor** - Morton K. Schwartz - A play about a girl's efforts to join a club.

86 **Haunted Castles** - A comprehension passage about haunted castles.

86 – 88 **The Red Room** - H.G. Wells - A ghost story about a haunted castle.

89 **Miracles** - Walt Whitman - A poem about the miracles of everyday life.

90 **Life on the Mississippi** - A factual article about the Mississippi river.

91 – 120 **Tom Sawyer** - Mark Twain - The classic novel about Tom's adventures with Huck Finn and Becky Thatcher.

97 **Schools in the 1840's** - A comprehension passage about schools in the time of Tom Sawyer.

106 **Trials** - A comprehension passage about trials.

Activities

Teacher-Directed Activities

The teacher-directed activities occur in the order listed below. The parentheses indicate activities that do not occur in every lesson.

- Word Practice Exercises
- Vocabulary Exercises
- (Skill Exercises)
- Group Reading
- Comprehension Questions
- Workcheck
- (Discussion Questions)

Independent Activities

The students do the activities listed below independently. The parentheses indicate activities that do not appear in every lesson.

- Silent Reading
- Workbook Items
- Skillbook Items
- (Special Project)

Sample Lesson

The following sample lesson shows the major components of the daily lessons.

The students begin every lesson by reading aloud from their *Skillbooks*. In part A, the students read lists of words that will appear in the stories. Exercises 1 – 3 in the *Presentation Book* provide instructions for presenting these lists.

In part B, the students learn the meanings of difficult words and phrases that will appear in the stories. Task B of Exercise 3 provides instructions for presenting these words.

PART A Word Lists

1	2	3
Le Maire	vessel	**Vocabulary words**
forecastle	cyclops	forecastle
hoist	Odyssey	skiff
Farallons	Dazzler	loot
photosynthesis		
sarcasm		
carnivores		
herbivores		

PART B New Vocabulary

1. **forecastle**—The **forecastle** is the part of the ship in which sailors sleep.
2. **skiff**—A **skiff** is a small rowboat.
3. **loot—Loot** is material that is stolen.
   - What do we call material that is stolen?*

EXERCISE 1 Word practice

*Pronunciation Guide: Forecastle—**Folk** sull*

1. Everybody, find lesson 59, part A in your skillbook. *Wait.* Touch under the words in column 1 as I read them.
2. The words in the first line are **Le Maire.**
3. Next word. **Forecastle.**
4. *Repeat step 3 for each remaining word in column 1.*
5. Your turn. Read the first line. *Signal.* **Le Maire.**
6. Next word. *Signal.* **Forecastle.**
7. *Repeat step 6 for each remaining word in column 1.*
8. *Repeat the words in column 1 until firm.*

EXERCISE 2 Word practice

1. Everybody, touch under the first word in column 2. *Pause.* What word? *Signal.* **Vessel.**
2. Next word. *Pause.* What word? *Signal.* **Cyclops.**
3. *Repeat step 2 for each remaining word in column 2.*
4. *Repeat the words in column 2 until firm.*

EXERCISE 3 Vocabulary development

Task A

1. Everybody, touch column 3.
   First you're going to read the words in column 3. Then you're going to read about what they mean.
2. Read the first word. *Signal.* **Forecastle.**
3. Next word. *Signal.* **Skiff.**
4. *Repeat step 3 for* ***loot.***
5. *Repeat the words in column 3 until firm.*

Task B

1. Everybody, look at part B. You're going to read that part out loud.
2. *Call on individual students to read each item aloud.*
   - *For questions followed by an asterisk, say:* "Everybody, what's the answer?"

   Key: **3. Loot**

In part C, the students review vocabulary words and practice using them in sentences. Exercise 4 provides instructions for presenting this review.

PART C Vocabulary Review

1	2
smirk	slender
crest	suppress
reveal	rebel

1. When you try to hold back an impulse, you __________ that impulse.
2. A sneer is a __________.
3. When you resist doing something you're expected to do, you __________.

EXERCISE 4 Vocabulary review

1. Everybody, look at part C. The words in the box are words you've learned.
2. Read the first word. *Signal.* **Smirk.**
3. Next. *Signal.* **Crest.**
4. *Repeat step 3 for the remaining words in the box.*
5. *Repeat the words in the box until firm.*
6. I'll read the items. When I come to a blank, everybody say the part that goes in the blank.
7. Look over item 1. *Pause.* Listen. When you try to hold back an impulse, you *Pause. Signal.* **suppress** that impulse.
8. *Repeat step 7 for each remaining item.*

Key: **2. smirk**
3. rebel

In part D, the students read a skill exercise. The skill exercises teach skills that are applied throughout the program. In this particular exercise, the students learn to identify sarcasm. Other skill exercises teach grammar, logic, and literary terms.

PART D Sarcasm

Sometimes people say the opposite of what they really mean. But they give evidence that they don't mean what they say. When people speak in that way, they are using **sarcasm.**

1. Here's an example of sarcasm:
   A boy says, "I just love going to school. I love to sit there all day long and do boring things. I love to work and study when I could be outside playing and swimming with nobody to tell me what to do."
   a. How does the boy *say* he feels about school? Ⓐ
   b. The boy gives evidence that contradicts what he says. Name something he says about school that contradicts the idea that he loves it. Ⓑ

EXERCISE 5 Sarcasm

1. Everybody, look at part D. *Check.*
2. *Call on individual students to read. Present the tasks specified for each circled letter.*

Ⓐ What's the answer? *Idea:* He loves it.
Ⓑ *Call on individual students.* Name one piece of evidence. *Ideas:* He does boring things; he could be playing.

After the students complete their *Skillbook* reading, they read from their *Textbooks*. In this sample lesson, the students begin their *Textbook* activities by reading a comprehension passage aloud. The comprehension passage provides background information for the day's story. Many *Textbook* stories and novels are preceded by comprehension passages.

The comprehension passage contains circled letters. As soon as the students read to a circled letter, the teacher presents comprehension questions specified in the *Presentation Book*.

EXERCISE 7 Comprehension passage

1. Everybody, turn to page 199 in your textbook.
2. *Call on individual students to read. Present the tasks specified for each circled letter.*

Ⓐ What is the name of the sloop? **The Dazzler.**
- Who wrote the novel about **The Dazzler? Jack London.**
- In which place does the novel begin? **San Francisco Bay.**
- Around what year? **1900.**

Ⓑ What's the answer? **Pacific Ocean.**
Ⓒ What's the answer? **San Francisco.**
Ⓓ What's the answer? **Oakland.**
Ⓔ What's the answer? **West.**

San Francisco Bay

Today, you will begin a short novel titled *The Cruise of the Dazzler*, by Jack London. *The Dazzler* is the name of a large sailboat called a sloop. The novel begins in San Francisco Bay around 1900. Ⓐ At that time, the bay was a very colorful place, with many seagoing vessels coming in and out of the bay. Some of these vessels carried passengers; some carried cargo; and some carried pirates who tried to steal cargoes from the other ships.

The map in the next column shows San Francisco Bay.

What is the name of the ocean near the bay? Ⓑ

What is the name of the city on the west side of the bay? Ⓒ

What is the name of the city on the east side of the bay? Ⓓ

In which direction would you go to get from Oakland to the Pacific Ocean? Ⓔ

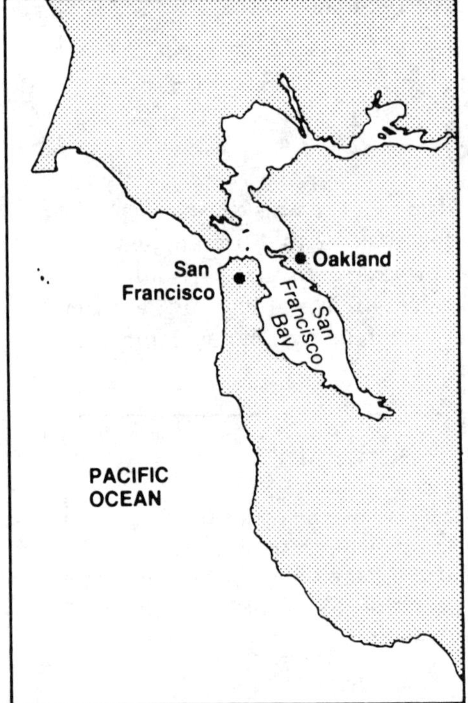

After they complete the comprehension passage, the students read the *find-outs* aloud. The *find-outs* appear at the beginning of most *Textbook* stories, and they alert the students to read for specific information.

After reading the *find-outs* aloud, the students usually read the rest of the story silently. The teacher then asks the comprehension questions specified in the *Presentation Book*. Many of these questions are based on the *find-outs*.

EXERCISE 8 Story reading

1. Everybody, turn to page 202.
2. *Call on individual students to read the title and the find-outs aloud. Then tell the students to read chapter 1 to themselves.*

After all students have finished reading:

- What is the name of the boat in this story? **The Dazzler.**
- What kind of sailboat is it? *Idea:* A sloop.
- What is the name of the boy who was experienced in sailing on that sloop? **Frisco Kid.**
- What is the name of the newcomer? **Joe Diaz.**
- What is the name of the captain of the sloop? *Idea:* Pete Le Maire.

CHAPTER 1

The New Boy

Find out:

- *The name of the boy who had experience sailing.*
- *The name of the new boy.*
- *The name of the captain.*
- *Where the new boy had come from.*
- *How the new boy felt about the other boy.*
- *What the men argued about.*

Frisco Kid was discontented—discontented and disgusted. He frowned, got up from where he had been sunning himself on the top of the *Dazzler*'s cabin, and kicked off his heavy rubber boots. Then he stretched himself on the narrow side deck and dangled his feet in the cool salt water.

Frisco Kid was discontented because he had to do more work than usual. He did not mind the cooking, nor washing down the decks. But when it came to the paint-scrubbing and dishwashing, he rebelled. He felt that he should not have to do that kind of work. After all, he knew how to handle the sails, lift anchor, steer, and make landings. That other work was for someone with less experience.

Suddenly, Frisco Kid heard a familiar voice ring out, "Stand out from under!" And Pete Le Maire, captain of the *Dazzler*, threw a bundle on deck and jumped aboard.

Then Pete shouted to the boy who owned that bundle. "Come! Queeck!" The boy hesitated on the dock. It was a good fifteen feet to the deck of the ship.

Pete smiled and said to the boy, "When I count three, jump on board. One, two, three!"

The boy threw his body into space and a moment later he struck the deck.

Pete addressed Frisco Kid. "Kid, dis is ze new sailor. I make your acquaintance." Pete smirked and bowed, and stood aside. "His name is Mistaire Joe Diaz," Pete said.

The two boys regarded each other silently for a moment. They were about the same age. Joe seemed to be the heartiest and strongest. Frisco Kid and Joe shook hands.

"So you're thinking of tackling the water, eh?" the Kid asked.

Joe Diaz nodded, and glanced around before answering. "Yes, I think the bay life will suit me for a while, and then when I've become used to it, I'm going to sea in the forecastle."

"In the what? In the *what*, did you say?"

"In the forecastle—the place where the sailors live," Joe explained, flushing and feeling unsure of his pronunciation.

On every lesson, the students answer written questions about that lesson's story. In this sample lesson, these questions appear in part A of the *Workbook* and part E of the *Skillbook*. The questions test the students' understanding of the critical details and themes of the story. Many questions require the students to use specific comprehension strategies taught in the skill exercises.

The students review and practice vocabulary words in every lesson. The students either use vocabulary words in sentence context or use them to complete crossword puzzles. In this sample lesson, vocabulary words are reviewed in part B of the *Workbook*.

WORKBOOK

PART A Story Items

1. a. What is the name of the boat in this novel? ____________
   b. What kind of sailboat is it? ____________
      • A sloop • A schooner • A steamer
   c. What is the name of the boy who was experienced in sailing on that sailboat? ____________
   d. What is the name of the newcomer? ____________
   e. How many years old is the newcomer? ____________
   f. What is the name of the captain of the sailboat? ____________
2. Joe said that he would like to go to sea in the forecastle. How is that word pronounced? ____________
   • fore-castle • folk-sull
   • for-sell
3. Here are some statements that Pete might make. Write what each statement means.
   a. "Come queeck!" ____________
   b. "Dis is ze new sailor." ____________
   c. "Leesen to what I say." ____________
   d. "Dese are ze sails, Joe." ____________
   e. "Are you feeling seeck?" ____________

PART B Vocabulary Items

Use the words in the box to fill in the blanks.

smarting	pertained to
reveal	trio
crest	absurd
slim	brave and noble
impudent	party
appealed to	

1. The ____________ woman charged into the burning house to save the baby.
   gallant
2. The fans arranged a ____________ for the new chess champion.
   reception
3. The ____________ barely squeezed into the back of the small car.
   group of three
4. She put the belt around her ____________ waist.
   slender
5. Only the turkey's ____________ poked out of the bushes.
6. The pirate parted the bushes to ____________ the gold statue.
7. The plan to plant more flowers only ____________ state parks.
   related to
8. My parents ____________ my sense of honesty, and convinced me to tell the truth.
   made an earnest request to

Specific skills are continuously reviewed. This continuous review enables the students to retain and master each new skill. In this sample lesson, parts F, G, and H of the *Skillbook* review specific skills.

Daily writing assignments require the students to write a paragraph on a specific topic. These assignments build writing skills and also allow the students to relate the stories to their personal experiences. In this sample lesson, the writing assignment appears in part I of the *Skillbook*.

PART E Story Items

1. **a.** What did the crew of the *Dazzler* sit on as they ate?
   b. The table in the cabin swung up on ______.
   c. Why was Joe impressed with Frisco Kid?
2. **a.** Twelve hours earlier, Joe Diaz had been a ______.
   b. When Joe thought of his mother, his feelings ______.
   • softened • hardened
   c. When Joe thought of his father, his feelings ______.
   • softened • hardened
   d. Which relative did Joe feel did not understand him?

PART F Drawing Conclusions

Write a conclusion that tells what the person believed.

1. *Neil believed that if you could speak French, you would gain power. Neil learned to speak French.*
- So, what did Neil believe would happen?

PART G Inference

Read the passage below and answer each question.

Photosynthesis

Plants and animals need food to survive, but they get their food in different ways. Animals must hunt for their food. Animals that eat plants must hunt for those plants. Animals that eat meat must hunt for other animals. They kill the animals and eat their meat.

Green plants are different. Green plants actually manufacture their own food. The leaves of the plant need three ingredients—sunlight, water, and carbon dioxide. Leaves convert these ingredients into food for the entire plant. Plants don't have to hunt for food. So long as a plant has sunshine, water, and carbon dioxide, the plant will manufacture its own food. This process is called ***photosynthesis.***

1. **a.** Name the three ingredients used by leaves to manufacture food for the entire plant.
   b. Is that question answered by **Words** or by a **Deduction?**
2. **a.** The process by which a plant manufactures its own food is called ______.
   b. **Words** or **Deduction?**
3. Write whether each living thing **hunts** for its food or **manufactures** its food:
   a. A giraffe
   b. An elm tree
   c. A snake

PART H Figurative Language

Write whether each statement is a **simile,** a **metaphor** or an **exaggeration.**

1. The day lasted forever.
2. The sound floated across the water.
3. Her cheeks were roses.

PART I Writing Assignment

Joe had many reasons for running away. Write a paragraph that explains his reasons. Tell what problems he had. Tell what he hoped would happen. Tell what might happen instead.

Make your paragraph at least **five** sentences long.

SKILLBOOK

General Information

Scheduling the Reading Period

Reading Mastery VI can be presented to the entire class or to smaller groups of students. The teacher-directed activities take about thirty minutes. The students need an additional thirty minutes during each lesson to complete their independent work. After the students have completed their independent work, the teacher conducts the workcheck, which takes about ten minutes. Here is one possible schedule for *Reading Mastery VI.*

8:45 – 9:15 Teacher-directed activities

9:15 – 9:45 Independent activities

9:45 – 9:55 Workcheck

The students can complete the independent activities in the *Skillbook* and *Workbook* immediately after the teacher-directed activities, or later in the school day, or as homework. The workcheck can be presented immediately after the students complete their independent work, or later in the day, or just before the next day's lesson.

If the class is divided into two groups, the teacher can work with one group while the other group is completing its independent work.

Using the Presentation Book

The *Presentation Book* contains complete scripts for presenting every lesson in *Reading Mastery VI.* The scripts are carefully written so that all teaching is clear and unambiguous. The program will be most effective if the scripts are followed closely.

The *Presentation Book* uses several typefaces:

- Type in color indicates what the teacher says.
- *This italic type indicates what the teacher does.*
- **This bold type indicates the students' answers to questions that require precise responses.**
- This light type indicates the basic idea of the students' answers to questions that permit varied responses.

Pacing the Lesson

The daily lessons should be presented at a lively pace. Fast pacing offers several advantages.

- Fast pacing keeps the students thinking. If a lesson is presented slowly, the students' minds may wander. With fast pacing, the students are constantly thinking, and they are unlikely to get distracted.
- Fast pacing encourages student achievement. With fast pacing, a teacher can cover more material and the students can receive more practice.
- Fast pacing reduces discipline problems. With fast pacing, the students are involved in their work and unlikely to misbehave.

To set a fast pace, the teacher should present the material quickly, but should not rush the students into making mistakes. Experience will determine the pace that is appropriate for each group. The teacher should read over the material before presenting it. Fast pacing is easier if the teacher does not have to refer to the *Presentation Book* for every word.

Using Signals

All of the word-practice tasks and some of the vocabulary tasks require the entire group to respond in unison. When the group responds in unison

- every student must initiate a response
- every student is able to practice the task
- the teacher can monitor every student
- the teacher can hear any incorrect answers and correct them immediately

In order for the students to answer in unison, the teacher must use a signal. By using a signal, the teacher eliminates the problem of one student leading the rest of the group.

The teacher should use the following procedure when signaling.

1. Ask the specified question.
2. Pause for about one second.
3. Clap, or use another auditory signal such as a tap or a finger snap. A signal that can be heard is necessary because the students are not looking at you but at what they are reading.
4. Listen to the group response and correct any errors.
5. Move quickly to the next question.

The one-second pause is very important. It clearly separates the question from the signal and ensures that every student sees or hears the signal. The pause should always last for about one second. When the pause is of a consistent length, the group is able to answer more effectively.

Teaching to Mastery

Every skill in *Reading Mastery VI* should be taught to mastery. When a skill is taught to mastery, every student in the group is able to perform the skill independently, without making any mistakes.

Teaching to mastery is of critical importance, because the students are constantly applying each new skill. When a skill is taught to mastery, the students are able to retain and apply the skill, and they are prepared to learn related skills. By teaching every skill to mastery, the teacher ensures that each student is able to succeed throughout the program.

Teaching Techniques

This section lists the activities in *Reading Mastery VI* and describes specific teaching techniques for each activity. By mastering the techniques, you will become an effective teacher of *Reading Mastery VI.* A description and rationale for each activity precedes the teaching techniques for that activity. This section also provides instructions for helping students with reading difficulties.

The activities for *Reading Mastery VI* are listed in the next column. They are listed in the order in which they occur in a lesson. Parentheses indicate activities that do not occur in every lesson.

- **Word Practice Exercises** - You present word practice exercises.
- **Vocabulary Exercises** - You present vocabulary exercises.
- **(Skill Exercises)** - You present exercises that teach specific comprehension, reference and study skills.
- **Oral Reading** - You direct the students as they read a poem, a comprehension passage, *find-outs*, or part of a story out loud.
- **Silent Reading** - The students read a story silently.
- **Comprehension Questions** - You present comprehension questions.
- **Independent Work** - The students work in their *Skillbooks* and *Workbooks.*
- **Writing Assignment** - The students complete a daily writing assignment.
- **Workcheck** - You conduct a workcheck of the the students independent work. The students record their points in the *Workbook* point boxes; you record their points on a Group Summary Chart.
- **(Discussion Questions)** - You conduct group discussions.
- **(Special Projects)** - The students work on special projects.

Word Practice Exercises

Each *Skillbook* lesson presents words that will soon appear in the stories. These words are organized into word lists. The students practice reading these lists so that they will be able to read the listed words accurately in the stories. You direct the students to read the words aloud and in unison.

There are three kinds of word lists: lists of words that are difficult to decode; lists of words that are phonetically regular; and lists of vocabulary words.

- For lists of words that are difficult to decode, you read the list aloud. The students then read the list.
- For each word that is phonetically regular, you ask "What word"? The students then read the word.
- For lists of vocabulary words, you direct the students to read each word. Later in the lesson, you present specified vocabulary exercises for each word.

Sample word lists and accompanying teacher material appear in the next column.

The words in column 1 are difficult to decode. You model the pronuciation of these words by reading each word aloud. Then the students read the words in column 1. Column 2 contains words that the students have read before and new words that are phonetically regular. The students read the words in column 2 without a teacher model. The words in column 3 are vocabulary words. The students also read these words without a teacher model. Later in the lesson, you will present vocabulary exercises for each word in column 3.

1	2	3
toucan	China	**Vocabulary words**
chintz	Asia	blot out
torrent	tidal	invader
	Catherine	merge
	Moses	torrent

EXERCISE 1 Word practice

*Pronunciation Guide: toucan—**two** can*

1. Everybody, find lesson 75, part A in your skillbook. *Wait.* Touch under each word in column 1 as I read it.
2. The first word is **toucan**.
3. Next word. **Chintz**.
4. *Repeat step 3 for **torrent**.*
5. Your turn. Read the first word. *Signal.* **Toucan**.
6. Next word. *Signal.* **Chintz**.
7. *Repeat step 6 for **torrent**.*
8. *Repeat the words in column 1 until firm.*

EXERCISE 2 Word practice

1. Everybody, touch under the first word in column 2. *Pause.* What word? *Signal.* **China.**
2. Next word. *Pause.* What word? *Signal.* **Asia.**
3. *Repeat step 2 for each remaining word in column 2.*
4. *Repeat the words in column 2 until firm.*

EXERCISE 3 Vocabulary development

Task A

1. Everybody, touch column 3. First you're going to read the words in column 3. Then you're going to read about what they mean.
2. Read the first line. *Signal.* **Blot out**.
3. Next word. *Signal.* **Invader**.
4. *Repeat step 3 for each remaining word in column 3.*
5. *Repeat the words in column 3 until firm.*

Directing Word Practice Exercises

Here are some techniques for effectively directing word practice exercises.

Maintain clear signals. For each column, you

1. Direct the students to look at a word.
2. Pause.
3. Say, "What word?" or "Next word."
4. Signal.

The students respond in unison. Use a clap or some other auditory signal to indicate when the students are to respond. Your signal should follow "What word?" or "Next word" by one second. The timing should always be the same—very rhythmical and predictable.

Position yourself so you can observe what the students are doing. Do not stand in front of the group as you present the word practice exercises. Instead, walk among the students. When you stand behind the students and look over their shoulders, you can see whether they are looking at the correct words, and you can hear their responses better than you can from the front of the room.

Focus on the students who are most likely to make mistakes. Stand behind one of these students as you present two or three words. Then move behind another one. Observe whether the students are

- looking at the appropriate words
- saying the words correctly
- responding on signal or merely waiting for others to lead them

Correct signal violations and slow responses. Although rules about responding on signal may seem trivial, they are important. Some students may wait for other students to say the words. Unless the students respond together, you won't know which students are having trouble, and you won't be able to correct their problems.

To correct students who respond too soon or too late, say, "You have to wait for the signal," or "You're late." Then repeat the task, praising the students who respond on signal. Make sure your signal is clear.

Correct monotone responses. The students may also respond in a monotonous tone. These responses may indicate that the students do not know the words they are reading or are merely copying other students' responses.

To correct slow or monotone responses, say, "That doesn't sound right. Say it the way you normally would." Then read the words in the column correctly. Make sure you read the words in a normal speaking voice and be sure your reading of the word list is well paced.

Repeat each word that is read correctly by the group. For example, immediately after the word *tidal* is read, say, "Yes, tidal." Sometimes students read words incorrectly and you don't hear their mistakes. If you routinely say each word after the students read it, you guard against the possibility that the students will think their misreadings are correct.

Correct all word-reading errors immediately. Even if only one student in the group makes an error, consider the response incorrect and correct it as soon as you hear the error. Use the following procedure to correct word-reading errors.

1. Say the word.
2. Direct the students to return to the first word in the column.
3. Read all the words in the column again.

The second step is very important. The students soon learn that they must remember how to read the words you have helped them with.

Treat the column as the unit of mastery. The objective is for the students to read all the words in each column quickly and without error. The unit of mastery is the column of words, not the individual word. The students must read all the words in a column without error before you present the next column. When the students master each column of words, they will be able to read those words in the stories.

Use individual turns. If you are unsure of individual responses, give the students individual turns reading the words in a column.

Establish a goal for good performance. If the students continue to make errors after you have corrected them, give them a goal—a reason for trying to perform well. Don't expect the students to stop making errors if you simply tell them that they are careless. Instead, set up the word practice exercises so that there is a reason for the students to perform well. Here are two techniques.

- **Use the present performance of the students to promote improvement.** For example,if the students usually need four repetitions of a column before they can read it without error, tell them that if they can master each column with only three repetitions, the group will earn bonus points. As the performance of the group improves, make a corresponding change in the requirement for earning bonus points. (See page 40 for a complete discussion of bonus points.)
- **Challenge the students.** In addition to using bonus points, express some doubt about the students' ability. Say, "I don't know whether you can read this list, because the words are very hard." When the students do well, express disbelief. Say, "I really didn't think you'd be able to read that list."

The two techniques described above work well in combination.

Work on your presentation. If the students continue to make mistakes when reading columns of words, there may be several problems. Possibly, the students are not motivated and are not trying to read accurately. Possibly, the students are trying to read rapidly rather than carefully. Possibly, there are problems with your presentation. Make sure you

- correct all errors immediately
- do not permit individual students to lead the group
- do not permit monotone responses
- use good pacing

If the students are still having problems after you have worked on your presentation, here are two possible solutions.

- Give the students more frequent individual turns.
- Introduce a reward for individual turns. For example, if each student who is called on for an individual turn reads without error, give everybody in the group bonus points.

Vocabulary Exercises

Reading Mastery VI teaches the meanings of more than 650 difficult vocabulary words and phrases. The program also provides extensive vocabulary practice so that the students can become facile in using the vocabulary words. All vocabulary words first appear in teacher-directed exercises for at least two consecutive lessons. The students then read the vocabulary words in the stories. Finally, the words are reviewed in the written vocabulary exercises and crossword puzzles that appear in the *Skillbook* and *Workbook*. The repeated appearance of vocabulary words in teacher-directed exercises, stories, and written exercises ensures student mastery of all vocabulary words.

The teacher-directed vocabulary exercises appear in the *Skillbook*. There are two types of exercise. The first type introduces new vocabulary words; the second type reviews old vocabulary words.

The Introductory Vocabulary Exercise

The introductory vocabulary exercise takes many forms. In the most common form, a student reads a word and its meaning out loud. The group then uses the word in context. Here is an example:

5. **cease**—Another word for **stop** is **cease.**
   a. What's another way of saying **The rain stopped?***
   b. What's another way of saying **Soon the battle will stop?***

The asterisk at the end of each question indicates that the teacher is to say, "Everybody, what's the answer"? The group then responds in unison. This unison group response requires every student to use the new word in context. The students not only learn the meaning of the new word but also receive practice in using the word. Word meaning becomes much more apparent to the students when this kind of practice occurs.

Sometimes, the questions do not require the group to use the word in context. Here is an example:

1. **canvas—Canvas** is a strong cloth that is used for sails.
   - What do we call a strong cloth that is used for sails?*

This form is used for words with long meanings, particularly nouns. For these words, recognition of the meaning is more important than using the word in context.

Some questions call for an individual response, rather than a group response. These questions typically have several correct answers. Here is an example:

5. **pluck**—When you **pluck** a plant from the ground, you quickly remove it from the ground.
   - What are you doing when you quickly remove a plant from the ground?

Note that the question is not followed by an asterisk, which means that the answer is given by an individual student. Correct answers might include, "plucking it," "plucking a plant, " or "plucking it from the ground."

Occasionally, a word meaning will not be followed by a question. This form is used for words that are easily remembered or that may already be familiar to the students. Here is an example:

2. **boar**—A **boar** is a wild pig that has long tusks.

The student simply reads the word meaning.

The Vocabulary Review Exercise

All vocabulary words are systematically reviewed. After a vocabulary word is introduced, it appears on the next lesson in a teacher-directed review exercise. Then the word appears in the stories. Finally, the word is reviewed in the independent work. The word *astronomer*, for example, is introduced on lesson 72. It appears in the teacher-directed review exercise on lesson 73, and in the story for lessons 73, 74 and 75. Finally, it is reviewed in the independent work in lessons 73, 74 and 75, as well as in subsequent lessons.

For the teacher-directed review exercise, the students use vocabulary words to complete sentences. The sentences define the meanings of the words.

A sample review exercise and its accompanyin teacher material appear in the next column. In the first part of the exercise, the students read the vocabulary words in unison. Then the teacher instructs the students to look over the first item. The teacher reads the first part of the item. In unison, the students say the word that goes in the blank. When necessary, the teacher reads the last part of the item after the students respond. The same procedure is repeated for each remaining item.

Later in the lesson, during the independent work, the students write the answers for this exercise.

1	2	3
writhes	astronomer	outwit
hurtled	overwhelms	unheeded
observatory	greeting	scorn

1. Something that overpowers you, ________ you.
2. Another word for **hate** is ________.
3. When something squirms and wiggles vigorously, it ________.
4. When you don't pay attention to something or don't notice it, that thing is ________.
5. A building that is designed to let people look at the stars is called an ________.
6. A person who studies the stars and planets is called an ________.

EXERCISE 3 Vocabulary review

1. Everybody, look at part C. The words in the box are words you've learned.
2. Read the first word. *Signal.* **Writhes.**
3. Next. *Signal.* **Hurtled.**
4. *Repeat step 3 for the remaining words in the box.*
5. *Repeat the words in the box until firm.*
6. I'll read the items. When I come to a blank, everybody say the part that goes in the blank.
7. Look over item 1. *Pause.* Listen. Something that overpowers you, *Pause. Signal.* **overwhelms** you.
8. *Repeat step 7 for each remaining item.*

Key: 2. **scorn**
3. **writhes**
4. **unheeded**
5. **observatory**
6. **astronomer**

The students also work another vocabulary review exercise during the independent work. This exercise is similar in form to the teacher-directed exercise, but the items are different. The students must use prompts or context clues in order to fill in the blanks. Here is an example:

Use the words in the box to fill in the blanks.

adorned	remote
squirmed	hateful
reception	obliged
forged ahead	observatory
frail	astronomer
heed	despises
overwhelmed	vengeance

1. The rancher ________________
really hates
wolves because they eat his cattle.

2. The trail was so ________________
far away
that it wasn't recorded on any of the maps.

3. Demeter ________________
moved forward with determination
in her search for her daughter.

4. Since they were still mad at me for the joke I played on them, they gave me a very cold ________________.
greeting

5. They did not ____________ the
attend to
woman's advice to stay close to the road.

6. The snake ____________ in
writhed
agony when the woman hit it with a rake.

Vocabulary words are also reviewed through crossword puzzles. These puzzles appear in the *Workbook*, and they resemble standard crossword puzzles, except that they only contain words taught in the program.

Presenting the Vocabulary Exercises

Instructions for presenting the vocabulary exercises appear in the *Presentation Book.* Here are some techniques that will help you teach the vocabulary exercise effectively.

Pace group-response tasks. The introductory vocabulary exercises often require group responses. For every question followed by an asterisk, you are to say, "Everybody, what's the answer?" Pause about two seconds before signaling the students to answer. The students often need thinking time to figure out the answer. If you require them to answer too quickly, you will rush some of them into making mistakes.

The teacher-directed review exercise also requires group responses. In this exercise, you pause before signaling the students to say the word that goes in the blank. Once again, be certain that the students have enough time to figure out the answer.

Make sure individual responses are heard by the group. For many vocabulary questions, only one student gives the answer. Make sure the entire group hears that student's answer.

Provide extra review for troublesome words. Take note of the vocabulary words that are still troublesome for the students after two teacher-directed exercises. Review these words in subsequent lessons and at other times during the school day.

Accept all correct student responses. Sometimes students give a secondary meaning of a word that is different from the meaning given in the vocabulary exercise. Accept all correct definitions and explain that some words have several meanings.

Skill Exercises

Reading Mastery VI teaches some comprehension, reference and study skills through specific skill exercises. Other comprehension skills are taught through the story questions, which are discussed on page 33 of this guide.

The specific skill exercises are presented cumulatively, which means that a particular skill is practiced repeatedly over several lessons, and then applied in later lessons. This cumulative practice ensures that the students apply the skills in a variety of contexts.

The list below shows the specific skill exercises for *Reading Mastery VI.* The numbers indicate the consecutive lessons on which a particular skill is taught and practiced. Once a skill is taught, it is intermittently reviewed throughout the program. For example, outlining is taught and practiced on lessons 15 through 28. Outlining is then intermittently reviewed through the program, appearing about once every five lessons.

- outlining: 15-28
- relevant information: 21-31
- contradictions: 32-42
- figurative language: 39-62
- inference: 54-63
- conversations: 61-67
- substitute and missing words: 66-75
- combined sentences: 74-83
- filling out forms: 81-84
- using reference materials: 85-90
- maps and graphs: 87-101
- irony: 88-92
- arguments: 94-120
- skills review: 30-120

Outlining

There are three types of outlining exercise. In the first type, the students write the main idea and supporting details for a single paragraph. These paragraphs are taken directly from the stories. The use of story material makes the exercise more relevant to the students and also reviews the stories. The students must use complete sentences and proper indentation when they write the main idea and supporting details.

The second type of outlining exercise gives the students three main ideas from a story they have read. These main ideas provide a broad outline of the story. The students must then write three or four supporting details for each main idea.

The third type of outlining exercise presents passages from the stories. The students write the main idea and supporting details for each paragraph in the passage.

Relevant Information

The ability to identify relevant information is an important thinking skill. The relevant information exercises teach the students to identify which information is relevant to a fact and which information is irrelevant. There are two types of exercise. In the first type, the students are given a fact and four statements. The students must then identify which statements are relevant to the fact and which statements are irrelevant. Here is an example:

> Write **relevant** or **irrelevant** for each item.
> - Fact: *The girl hammered a nail into a piece of wood.*
>
> 1. She had yellow hair. ____________
> 2. She was building a dog house. ____________
> 3. She was putting on the roof of the house. ____________
> 4. Her dog was named Spot. ____________

In the second type of relevant-information exercise, the students are given two facts and four statements. They must then identify which statements are relevant to the first fact, which statements are relevant to the second fact, and which statements are irrelevant to both facts.

Contradictions

The contradictions exercises teach the students how to identify contradictory statements in a text. There are three types of exercise. The first type presents a true statement and a contradictory statement. The students must explain, in writing, how the contradictory statement contradicts the true statement. Their explanation must be in the form of an "if-then" statement. Here is an example:

> 1. Assume that this statement is true: *Libby loved all vehicles.* Then this statement is a contradiction: *Libby hated motor scooters.*
>   - Fill in the blanks to tell why the statement is a contradiction.
>   If __________, then __________.

In the second type of contradictions exercise, the students are presented with a passage. One of the sentences in the passage is underlined. The students must find a sentence in the passage that contradicts the underlined sentence. Then they explain the contradiction in writing.

The third type of contradictions exercise also presents a passage, but without an underlined statement. The students identify the contradictory statements and then explain the contradiction in writing. Here is an example:

> Read the passage below and find a statement that contradicts an earlier statement.
> *Many people are changing the way they eat. Rock star Biff Socko says, "I no longer eat any kind of bread. Bread is bad for you and hurts your voice." Every day, Biff has grapes and cucumbers for breakfast. Then he eats a large whole wheat roll. He has been eating this way for a long time.*
> 1. Underline the statement you assume to be true.
> 2. Circle the contradiction.
> 3. Write an **if-then** statement that explains the contradiction.

Figurative Language

The students learn to recognize and interpret four types of figurative language: similes, metaphors, exaggeration and sarcasm. Many of the exercises use examples taken directly from the stories. This strategy allows the students to apply their skills while reading the stories, which leads to greater comprehension.

Each type of figurative language is taught separately. The students first learn about similes. The initial similes exercise teaches the students how to analyze a simile. The students identify which two things a simile compares, and then they explain how those things are the same. Here is an example:

> **1.** *The miner's hands looked like a lump of coal.*
> **a.** What two things are the same in that simile?
> **b.** How could those things be the same?
> **c.** Name two ways those things are different.

A subsequent similes exercise teaches the students how to write their own similes. The students are given a literal statement, such as *His heart had no feeling.* They then name something that has no feeling, such as iron. Finally, the students use what they have named in order to write a simile: for example, "His heart was like iron."

The metaphor exercises are similar to the simile exercises. The students identify which two things are compared in a metaphor and then explain, in writing, how those two things are the same.

The exaggeration exercise teaches the students that exaggerations try to stretch the truth. The students identify which part of an exaggeration stretches the truth, and then they rewrite the exaggeration so that it does not stretch the truth. Here is an example:

> Exaggeration is another type of figurative language. When you exaggerate, you try to stretch the truth. You say that something is bigger or faster or longer than it really is.
>
> **1.** Here's an example of exaggeration: *Frank worked for a year that afternoon.*
> **a.** How long does the statement say that Frank worked?
> **b.** Could Frank really have worked that long in the afternoon?
> **c.** What part of the statement stretches the truth?
> **d.** Use accurate language to tell what the exaggeration means.

In the sarcasm exercise, the students learn that sarcasm occurs when people say the opposite of what they really mean. The exercise presents a passage that contains a sarcastic statement. The students identify the sarcastic statement and then use evidence from the passage to explain, in writing, why the statement is sarcastic.

Inference

The ability to make inferences is essential for good reading comprehension. There are two types of inference exercise. The first type teaches the students deductive logic, which is the basis of inference. In this exercise, the students complete deductions and practice saying entire deductions. Here is an example:

> Complete each deduction.
> 1. Here's the evidence:
> *Every bird has feathers.*
> *A heron is a bird.*
> • What's the conclusion about a heron?Ⓐ
>
> ---
>
> **EXERCISE 5** Deductions
> 1. Everybody, look at part D. *Check.*
> When you use evidence to draw a conclusion, you're completing a **deduction.** What are you doing? **Completing a deduction.**
> 2. *Call on individual students to read. Present the tasks specified for each circled letter.*
> Ⓐ Say the conclusion about a heron.
> **A heron has feathers.**
> Listen to the whole deduction:
> **Every bird has feathers.**
> **A heron is a bird.**
> **Therefore, a heron has feathers.**
> Everybody, say the whole deduction. *Signal.*
> *The students respond together. Repeat until firm.*

The students first complete the deduction by drawing a conclusion about a heron: "A heron has feathers." Then they say all the parts of the deduction out loud. All of the deductions follow the classic rule-instance-conclusion form.

The second type of inference exercise requires the students to apply what they have learned about deductions. The exercise presents an expository passage and a group of questions. Some of the questions can be answered by specific words in the passage. Other questions can only be answered by completing a deduction. The students read the passage and answer the questions. Then they indicate whether each question is answered by words in the passage or by a deduction.

Conversations

Narrative prose often involves conversations between unidentified speakers.

There are two types of conversations exercise.

The first type presents dialogues in which the speakers are not always identified. The students must use internal evidence to identify which person makes each statement in the dialogue. Here is an example:

> Below is a conversation between Harumi and Yoshio. Write which person makes each statement.
>
> Harumi, a twelve year old girl, was glad to see her brother. "Yoshio," she said, "I can't believe that you are finally home."① She paused a moment, and smiled. "Is college really difficult?" she asked.②
>
> "Oh, I think sixth grade was harder, because of Mrs. Ozu."③
>
> "Yes, she is a very tough teacher. I am in her class now."④
>
> "I know," Yoshio observed. "You told me in your letter."⑤ "Tell me," he asked, "does she still give a test every day?"⑥
>
> "Not only that, but she won't give us any recess if we make too much noise."⑦

In the second conversations exercise, the students are provided with descriptions of different characters, followed by several statements. The students then write which character could have made each statement.

Substitute and Missing Words

Adult-level writing makes extensive use of pronouns and other referents. Sometimes, referents can be quite obscure; at other times, they may not even appear. The substitute and missing words exercises teach the students how to interpret referents and how to supply missing referents. There are two types of substitute word exercises and one type of missing word exercise.

The first type of substitute word exercise presents sentences that contain substitute words, such as pronouns and adverbs. The substitute words are underlined. The students must identify the word that each substitute word replaces.

Sometimes, a referent may refer to an entire sentence or to a group of sentences. The second type of substitute word exercise teaches the students how to interpret these referents. The exercise presents a passage in which a single substitute word is underlined. The students must circle all the sentences that the substitute word refers to. Then they write the main idea of those sentences. Here is an example:

> Sometimes words refer to a whole sentence or a whole passage. Below is an example.
>
> *Both hooks were thrown overboard together, and seventy feet of line whizzed out. Joe instantly felt the struggling jerks of a hooked fish. As he began to haul the fish in, he glanced at Frisco Kid, and saw that he, too, had captured a fish on his line. The race between them was exciting. Hand over hand, the wet lines flashed on board. It was royal sport.*
>
> The underlined word is **it.** That word refers to all the things about Joe's fishing.
> 1. Draw one circle around all the sentences that tell what **it** was.
> 2. Write the main idea that tells what **it** was.

The missing word exercise presents sentences that are shortened. Here is an example:

> For each sentence below, make an arrowhead like this ∧ in the sentence to show each place words are missing. Then write the missing words above the arrowhead.
>
> 1. Although Nora has blue eyes, her
>
>   sister doesn't.

The students indicate where words are missing, and then they write those words. The completed first sentence, for example, would be, "Although Nora has blue eyes, her sister doesn't have blue eyes."

Combined Sentences

The combined sentence exercises teach the students how to interpret sentences that use apposition. There are two types of combined sentence exercise. The first type presents a pair of sentences, such as: *The toucan has bright feathers. The toucan is a tropical bird.* The first sentence introduces an unfamiliar word - *toucan* - and the other sentence tells what the word means. The students learn to combine the sentences so that the meaning is in apposition with the unfamiliar word: "The toucan, a tropical bird, has bright feathers."

In the second type of combined sentence exercise, the students read sentences that make use of apposition. The students must identify the appositive and the word it modifies. Here is an example:

> 1. Below is a combined sentence that presents a new word and tells what that new word means. The new word is not underlined.
>
> - *Luigi played the ocarina, a small wind instrument.*
>   - **a.** What is the new word?
>   - **b.** What does the new word mean?
>   - **c.** What else does the sentence tell about the new word?

Filling Out Forms

The filling-out-forms exercise presents a group of facts followed by a series of questions typically found on forms. The students use the facts to answer the questions. Here is an example:

> Use the facts to fill out the form.
>
> **Facts:** *Your name is Homer Price. You are sixteen years old. You are applying for a job at a factory that makes doughnut machines. You know how the machines work, and you have fixed them before. You live at 417 Central Street, in Centerburg, Ohio.*
>
> **1.** Name: ____________________
>
> **2.** Age: ____________________
>
> **3.** Full Address: ____________________
>
> ____________________
>
> **4.** What qualifications do you have for this job?
>
> **a.** ____________________
>
> ____________________
>
> **b.** ____________________
>
> ____________________

Reference Skills

The reference skills exercises teach the students how to use reference materials and how to read for specific information. There are two types of reference skills exercises. In the first type, the students learn the functions of atlases, encyclopedias and dictionaries. The students then identify which reference book they would use to find different kinds of information. Here is an example:

> There are several kinds of reference books you can use to find information.
>
> An **atlas** gives facts about places. It shows the size of cities and countries. It shows how far it is from one place to another. It tells how many people live in different places.
>
> An **encyclopedia** gives facts about nearly everything. It tells about planets and plants, about animals and buildings, and about history and famous people.
>
> A **dictionary** gives facts about words. It shows how to spell a word and how to pronounce it. It tells what part of speech a word is and what the word means. A dictionary also tells the history of words.
>
> - Which reference book would you use to find each of the following pieces of information?
>
> **1.** How to spell the word *doughnut.*
> **2.** How far it is from Denver to Kansas City.
> **3.** What Duke Ellington is famous for.
> **4.** When the Civil War took place.
> **5.** How many people live in Mexico City.
> **6.** How to pronounce the word *succinct.*

The second type of reference skills exercise presents reference material. The students answer questions about the material.

Maps and Graphs

The students receive extensive practice in interpreting maps and graphs. Maps appear in many of the stories, and questions about those maps are integrated with the story questions. In addition to these questions, there are two types of map skill exercises. The first type of exercise presents a map and a series of questions about the map. These questions involve direction, relative size, proximity, and interpretation of legends.

The second type of exercise presents a map and a group of statements about the map. Some of these statements contradict the map. The students must write *contradictory* or *not contradictory* for each statement. An example appears in the next column.

Assume that the map below is accurate. Examine the map carefully, and then read the statements below it. Some of the statements contradict what is shown on the map. Write **Contradictory** or **Not contradictory** for each statement.

1. New Orleans is south of Memphis.
2. The Mississippi flows into the Gulf of Mexico.
3. Saint Louis is in the state of Missouri.
4. The Mississippi touches twelve states.
5. Arkansas is north of Iowa.

The graph exercises are similar to the map exercises. The first type of graph exercise presents a graph and a series of questions about the graph. Here is an example:

> The graph below shows how much snow falls in the Red Hills. The numbers along the side tell how many centimeters of snow fell in a year. The numbers along the bottom tell how many meters high the hills are.
>
> 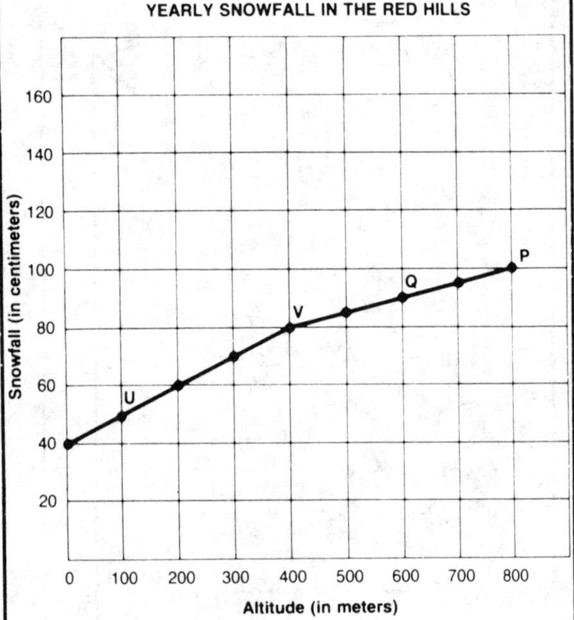
>
>
> 1. The letter **V** shows how many centimeters of snowfall occur at a certain altitude.
>   **a.** Which altitude?
>   **b.** How much snowfall?
> 2. Was there more snowfall at the **higher altitudes** or the **lower altitudes?**
> 3. Which point tells about a higher altitude, **U** or **P?**
> 4. How many centimeters of snow fell on hills that had an altitude of 800 meters?

The second type of graph exercise presents a graph and a series of statements about the graph. The students write *contradictory* or *not contradictory* for each statement.

Irony

Irony is an important literary device, and many of the stories in the program make use of irony. The irony exercises teach the students how to recognize and interpret irony. The students first learn that irony is the result of a chain of events.

- A character believes something.
- The character does things that are based on the belief.
- Later, the character finds out that the belief was mistaken.

The students then practice identifying this chain of events within stories they have read. The story *The Necklace*, for example, tells about a woman named Matilda who loses a necklace that she believes is valuable. Matilda buys a new necklace and then spends ten years paying for it. At the end of the story, Matilda finds out that the original necklace was really a worthless fake. Here is the irony exercise for *The Necklace.*

> Here's how irony works:
> - A character believes something.
> - The character does things that are based on the belief.
> - Later, the character finds out that the belief was mistaken.
>
> Here's an example of irony from *The Necklace:*
> 1. Matilda had a mistaken belief about the necklace. What was that?
> 2. Matilda did something that was based on that belief. What did she do?
> 3. What would she have done if she had known the truth about the necklace?

In this exercise, the students not only identify the ironic chain of events, but also speculate on other narrative possibilities.

Arguments

The last group of skill exercises teaches the students how to recognize faulty arguments. The students learn seven rules for identifying faulty arguments. Each rule refutes a particular type of faulty argument. Here is a list of the rules.

- Just because two things happen around the same time doesn't mean one thing causes the other thing.
- Just because you know about a part doesn't mean you know about the whole thing.
- Just because a person is an expert in one field doesn't mean the person is an expert in another field.
- Just because the writer presents some choices doesn't mean that there are no other choices.
- Just because you know about the whole thing doesn't mean you know about every part.
- Just because two words sound the same doesn't mean they have the same meaning.
- Just because you know about one part doesn't mean you know about another part.

Here is the exercise that teaches the first rule.

> Here's a rule: *Just because two events happen around the same time doesn't mean one event causes the other event.*
>
> The following argument breaks the rule.
>
> "The last five times Joe tapped home plate, he hit a home run. He should always remember to tap home plate when he goes up to bat."
>
> **1.** What two events happen around the same time?
> **2.** What event does the writer think causes the home run?

The exercises for the remaining rules are similar. First the rule is presented, and then it is applied to a faulty argument. The students demonstrate their understanding of the rule by answering the questions.

There is also an arguments exercise that reviews all the rules. This exercise presents several faulty arguments. The students must identify which rule each argument breaks.

Procedures for Teaching Skill Exercises

Teach the skill exercises as indicated in the *Presentation Book.* New skills are usually presented in a series of exercises that occur over several lessons. The students are taught the skill and are then provided with practice in applying the skill to different examples. Here are some techniques for ensuring student mastery of the skills.

Observe independent work performance. The students should be able to master each new skill within two or three lessons. If the students are having problems with a skill after this time, these problems should be corrected immediately.

Reteach the skill. After the workcheck, assemble the students who are having trouble. Repeat the exercises from the *Presentation Book* that teach the skill. Present individual turns to each student, and reassign the skill items that appear in the *Skillbook* or *Workbook.* Make sure you let the students know they will be using the skill in later lessons.

Award bonus points. If the students have serious problems, award bonus points to all students who do the newly taught skill exercises in the *Workbook* or *Skillbook* without error. (See page 40 for a complete discussion of bonus points.)

Oral Reading

Oral reading is a part of every lesson in *Reading Mastery VI.* During the teacher-directed *Skillbook* exercises, the students read word lists, vocabulary exercises and some skill exercises orally. After the students complete these activities, they read in the *Textbook.* Each *Textbook* lesson includes some oral reading. The students read all the comprehension passages, poems, plays and *find-outs* aloud, as well as parts of many stories. This section describes the procedures for conducting oral reading in the *Textbook.*

Comprehension Passages

Many stories are preceded by comprehension passages that the students read aloud. These passages present background information about the setting, the events, or the characters of a story. This background information helps the students to understand the stories more fully.

The comprehension passages contain circled letters. You call on different students to read several sentences aloud. At each circled letter, you present comprehension questions specified in the *Presentation Book.* (Techniques for presenting these questions are discussed on page 33).

The students must demonstrate a thorough understanding of the information presented in the comprehension passages, because they will be using that information as they read the stories. If the students make frequent errors when answering the comprehension questions, repeat the questions after the students have finished reading the passage.

Find-outs

Beginning on lesson 21, each story is preceded by a group of *find-outs* that the students read aloud. The *find-outs* alert the students to important elements of the story they are about to read. Here are the *find-outs* for the first chapter of *Sara Crewe.*

> *Find out:*
> - *Where Miss Minchin lived.*
> - *What Sara was like.*
> - *What Captain Crewe bought for Sara.*
> - *How Sara felt about Miss Minchin.*

You call on different students to read the *find-outs* aloud. Many of the comprehension questions are based on the *find-outs,* so the students should pay close attention during this reading.

Reading Stories Aloud

The students read the first part of many stories aloud, as well as the play and all of the poems. The first part of every story in lessons 1-20 is read aloud. This emphasis on reading stories aloud early in the program helps build the students' decoding skills for later lessons. After lesson 20, about one fourth of the lessons include some oral story reading.

The part of the story the students are to read aloud starts with the title and continues to the last circled letter. You call on different students to read three to five sentences. At each circled letter, you present the comprehension questions specified in the *Presentation Book.* (Techniques for presenting these questions are discussed on page 33.)

The first ten *Textbook* lessons have a decoding error limit. This limit is based on one decoding error per seventy words in the story. If the students finish the oral reading and stay within the error limit, you award the group two points for good reading. The students record their points in the box labeled **R** at the top of their *Workbook* lesson.

If the group exceeds the error limit, tell them that

- they must reread the oral reading section of the lesson
- each student will earn one point for the rereading if the group meets the error limit
- you will present no comprehension questions during the rereading

Try to schedule the rereading as soon as possible. If there is time in the period, start the rereading immediately. The students should not begin the silent reading and the independent work until they have read the oral reading section within the error limit.

Conducting Oral Reading

Position yourself. If the group is large, circulate among the students as they read and observe them from behind. You will be able to observe them better from behind than from the front. Spend most of your time near the below-average students but move around enough to let all the students know that you are observing them.

Make sure you receive a frequent sample of each student's oral reading. Oral reading is especially important for students who are not very fluent readers. If there are many students in your class, time may not permit you to call on each student to read every day. Make sure each student is called on every other day.

Do not call only on the students who read very well. All students should be given oral reading practice.

Do not overlook errors. Make it very clear to the students that if they exceed the error limit, they must reread the first part of the lesson.

Tell the students to read carefully. Tell the fast readers who are making errors to slow down. Remind the students of the points they will earn if the group doesn't go over the error limit.

Respond to the students' efforts as they are reading. Give them feedback from time to time, particularly if they are obviously trying to read carefully. If the students seem to hurry or guess, remind them of the error limit rules.

Make sure that the students follow along as others are reading. You can use two techniques that will encourage the students to follow along.

1. *Award bonus points for catching errors.* The students raise their hands when they hear an error. Call on one of them to identify the error. If the student is correct, award a bonus point to that student.
2. *The students lose their turn if they don't have their place when they're called on.*

Encourage less able readers to point to the words that are being read. By pointing, the students practice reading throughout the group reading. If they don't point, they may practice only when they are reading aloud. Think of the pointing as a way of maximizing practice.

Recognize common decoding errors. Here is a list of common decoding errors.

- *Leaving off an ending.* Saying *look* for *looked* is an error. Saying *run* for *runs* is an error.
- *Saying the wrong word.* Saying *a* for *the* is an error. Saying *what* for *that* is an error.
- *Repeated self-corrections.* A self-correction occurs when a student says the wrong word and then rereads the word correctly. If a student makes continual self-corrections, count all self-corrections as errors. However, if there are only occasional self-corrections, do not count them as errors.
- *Word omissions or insertions.* If a students frequently omits or adds words to sentences, count the omissions and insertions as errors.
- *Repeated line-skipping.* Like self-corrections, occasional line-skipping should not be treated as an error. Simply tell the student to move up to the appropriate line and reread the entire sentence. However, if line-skipping occurs frequently, count each occurence as one error.
- *Repeated partial reading.* If a student usually reads sentences in this manner: *They went with - went with - the boys from - the boys from town*, count one error. Occasional rereadings to fix the phrasing of a sentence are acceptable. Chronic rereading, however, should be treated as an error.
- *Repeated word-part or syllable reading.* If a student usually pronounces longer words a syllable at a time before saying the word, the student is making decoding errors. Count each chronic occurence as one error.

Correcting Decoding Errors

Use the following procedure for correcting all decoding errors during oral reading throughout the program.

1. Stop the student as soon as you hear the error. Do not wait for the student to finish the sentence.
2. Identify the error. Say, "You skipped a line," or "You left out a word," or "You repeated a word." For misidentified words, simply say the word and ask the student to repeat it. For example, say, "That word is **doughnut**. What word?"
3. Tell the student to read the sentence from the beginning.

The last step is particularly important. If the student correctly reads the sentence in which the error occurred, the student demonstrates that the correction was effectively communicated. If the student makes the same mistake or a different one when rereading the sentence, count the mistake as an additional error and repeat the correction procedure until the student reads the sentence correctly.

Working With Students Who Are Not Proficient in Oral Reading

Students who have not completed *Reading Mastery V* may be poor at oral reading and may consistently make decoding errors. Use the following procedures to help these students improve their oral reading.

Each day before beginning the oral reading, caution the students to read carefully. Sometimes students have the impression that they should read as fast as they can say the words. Tell these students to slow down and read accurately.

Award bonus points for good oral reading. If the students are having problems with the oral reading, use bonus points as an incentive. At the beginning of the oral reading, tell the students that they can earn bonus points if they make no errors.

Read long passages with individual students. Often, a student who is weak in decoding will tend to make a greater number of errors when reading long passages. You can take turns with the student. You read a few lines and the student reads the next few lines.

Require the students to catch your deliberate mistakes. With this procedure, you read somewhat haltingly and make mistakes from time to time. The student is to catch these mistakes. By reading haltingly, you make it possible for the student to follow along. By requiring the student to catch your mistakes, you ensure that the student is attending to the words even when not reading aloud.

Silent Reading

The students read most of the *Textbook* lessons silently. When the students complete their silent reading, you present the comprehension questions specified in the *Presentation Book.* (Specific techniques for presenting these questions are discussed on page 33.)

During silent reading, the students must read accurately and with good understanding. Here are some techniques for helping students develop good silent reading strategies.

Watch the students as they read, and make comments. For example, say, "Show me where you're reading. You're getting to a very interesting part."

Remind the students that you will ask them questions about what they read. Tell the students that they will be able to answer the questions if they read carefully.

Require the class to be silent during silent reading. If the students talk to each other during this time, tell them they can earn bonus points for remaining silent.

Have the students who finish early begin the writing assignment. Some students will complete the silent reading sooner than other students. The students who finish early can begin the writing assignment. They should wait until after you present the comprehension questions to begin the other exercises. Occasionally you may have to present the comprehension questions before every student has completed the silent reading. If so, the students who have not finished reading should stop reading, listen to the comprehension questions, and then complete the silent reading.

Comprehension Questions

The teacher presents comprehension questions during the group reading and after the silent reading. These questions involve literal and inferential comprehension, sequencing, supporting evidence, cause and effect, information-recall and other comprehension skills. There are also questions about character development, viewpoint, setting, plot, and theme. Additional comprehension skills are taught in the skill exercises, which have already been discussed.

Presenting the Comprehension Questions

The comprehension questions are specified in the *Presentation Book.* These questions are always presented to individual students. Here are some techniques for effectively presenting the questions.

During oral reading, present the specified questions as soon as the student who is reading aloud comes to a circled letter. Do not wait until the end of the story to present the comprehension questions.

You may add comprehension questions. If the students have problems with a particular concept, add a question about that concept. If the students have their own questions about the story, answer them, but do not become routinely sidetracked into long discussions. Occasionally you may want to reserve time for a discussion of stories that are particularly interesting to the students.

Accept appropriate answers for questions. Questions that are followed by an answer in bold-face type are to be answered exactly as indicated. For example:

Questions that are followed by the word *Idea(s)* are to be answered in the student's own words. An appropriate answer expresses the right idea, regardless of the specific words used in the *Presentation Book.* For example:

Correct errors immediately. When a student makes a mistake on a comprehension question, immediately indicate that the answer is wrong. Then call on another student to answer the question. When possible, have students find the specific sentence in the story that answers the question.

Present difficult questions twice. When a student makes a mistake on a difficult comprehension question, correct the error and mark the question in your *Presentation Book.* After you correct the error, say, "I'm going to ask that question later, so remember the answer." At the end of the comprehension questions, present any questions you marked.

If the students have trouble with certain comprehension questions, set up special challenges for the group. For example, after correcting a wrong answer, tell the students that you will have one student answer the question later. If that student answers the question correctly, everybody in the group will receive bonus points.

Independent Work

As part of every lesson, the students work independently for about thirty minutes, completing all of the *Workbook* and *Skillbook* exercises for that lesson. The students complete

- vocabulary items
- review items
- skill exercises
- questions about the *Textbook* stories
- writing assignments

Most of the *Skillbook* and *Workbook* exercises relate directly to the *Textbook* readings. This direct relationship demonstrates to the students that their readings are both important and useful. The students are rewarded for reading with good comprehension and for remembering what they read.

Directions for Independent Work

When the students complete the *Textbook*, they should start working in the *Workbook*, and then go on to the *Skillbook*.

The students write answers for *Workbook* items in the *Workbook*. They write answers for *Skillbook* items on their own sheet of lined paper. They should write their name on the paper, as well as the lesson number and the item number for each answer.

The students should not be permitted to look up answers in the *Textbook* when doing the independent work. Although the students develop skill in looking things up by referring back to the *Textbook*, the practice may prevent them from developing important strategies for organizing and remembering information. For example, the independent work often requires the students to arrange a list of story events in the correct order. Students who have trouble with these items have an inadequate strategy for organizing events. You will not learn about their inadequate strategies if they are permitted to look up the answers.

Most of the more difficult items that appear in the independent work have been presented as vocabulary and comprehension questions. If the students are not permitted to look up the answers, they will pay attention to your presentation of vocabulary and comprehensions questions and will remember the answers to important questions.

Monitoring Students as They Work Independently

Plan to observe the students during the independent work for about five minutes each day and possibly for a longer period during the first twenty lessons. You should walk around the classroom and observe the students as they work.

First observe the below-average students. Identify specific problems these students have. If a common problem emerges, such as misinterpreting an item or not knowing the answer for a particular item, look at the papers of some of the above-average students. If many students are having the same problem, stop the class and straighten out the problem. For example, say, "Many students are not reading item six carefully." If only a few students are having the problem, plan to remedy it during the workcheck.

Here is a checklist that will help you identify independent work problems.

Are the students skipping items? If so, say, "Check your work and make sure you have completed every item."

Are the students reading items correctly? As part of answering correctly, the students must read items correctly. Often it is possible to infer how a student misread an item from the student's answer. For example, one items asks: *Why couldn't Odysseus and his men move that door*? Some students may answer, "Yes." These students probably misread the item as, *Did Odysseus and his men move that door*? Tell these students to read the item again.

Are the students working without help? A major purpose of the *Workbook* and *Skillbook* exercises is to develop student ability to work independently. The more you help the students the less you know about what the students actually know and the more the students will rely on your help. You shouldn't help a student more than once during a lesson.

Are the students working at a reasonable rate? Students who are not well practiced in working independently often don't use their time well. To help the students use their time well, tell them how much time has passed and how much time they have left. If the students tend to work slowly, award bonus points for completing the independent exercise in a specified time period.

Do the students get stuck on a particular item? Students who have trouble with a particular item may not have a strategy for completing the page and then returning to a problem item. Tell these students that they should circle the problem item, complete the other items, and then return to the problem item later.

Are the answers to items correct? If not, tell the student, "Your answer to item 5 is not correct." You should not tell the student the answer, and you should not give this kind of help more than once for each student during a lesson.

Writing Assignments

Writing assignments are a part of every lesson. Many of the writing assignments ask the students to make judgments about important story events and to use evidence from the story to support their judgments. In addition, the students compare one story with another, make predictions, and express opinions.

Presenting and Grading the Assignments

Lessons 1-3 include detailed instructions for presenting the writing assignments. The instructions direct you to read the assignment aloud and ask questions related to the assignment. You also read and discuss examples of good writing.

Questions are included in the student material for all writing assignments from lessons 1-34. The questions provide the students with a means of organizing their thoughts and checking their completed assignments. After lesson 34, the questions are dropped.

The students can earn up to two bonus points for their writing assignments. Award bonus points based on how well the students are supporting their ideas, conclusions or opinions with evidence from the stories. Do not take off points for poor grammar or spelling. The main focus of the writing assignments is on getting students to think in writing; too much emphasis on grammar or spelling would inhibit this important skill.

Workcheck

The workcheck is a group activity. It should be conducted after the group has completed the independent work activities and before the next lesson is presented. Workchecks can be conducted right after the students finish their independent work, at another time during the day, or just before teaching the next day's lesson. (The workcheck will be the opening event of the next day's lesson if the students do their independent work as homework.) The workcheck takes from five to ten minutes.

The answer keys for the *Skillbook* and *Workbook* appear at the end of each lesson in the *Presentation Book.* Although how the workcheck is presented will vary from classroom to classroom, the following events should occur during each workcheck.

- All written answers should be checked.
- All incorrect answers should be marked with a checkmark and all correct answers should be marked with a **C**.
- The students should correct their incorrect answers.
- You should read and grade the writing assignments.
- You should award points according to the number of errors each student makes.
- You should provide a final check of each paper after the students have corrected their answers.

Presenting Workchecks

The students may check their own papers during the workcheck, or they may trade papers. Or, you may want to check the papers yourself.

The fastest procedure for going through the workcheck is for you to read each item and the correct answer. Students who have questions may raise their hands. If several students have questions about a particular item, tell them to mark the item with a question mark and that you will check those answers later. Then move quickly to the next item.

As you read the questions and give the answers, circulate among the students. Make sure they are marking each response with a checkmark or a **C**. By circulating among the students, you will discourage the students' tendency to change their answers without first marking the items.

After you have given the answers to all the items, tell the students to total their errors. Then tell them how many points they have earned for their independent work. (The point schedule is near the end of each lesson in the *Presentation Book.*) The students write their points for independent work in the box labelled **IW** that appears at the top of the *Workbook* lesson.

Give the students time to correct their papers. They should look up the correct answers in the *Textbook* and should use the glossary to look up vocabulary words they missed.

Determining Errors

Use the following criteria when correcting the independent work.

Count the total number of scoreable responses. Some items have both numbers and letters. Here is an example:

> **1. a.** Sylvia went to the large tree __________ in the morning.
> • early • late
> **b.** To climb the pine tree, Sylvia first climbed an __________ tree.
> **c.** Why did Sylvia climb the pine tree?
> **d.** What would be Sylvia's reward if she gave information to the stranger?

A student's answer for each part of this item is a scoreable response. Each response is marked either as correct or incorrect; therefore, the student makes four scoreable responses on this single item.

Some items have only one number but call for several responses. Here is an example:

> Put the following story events in the right order by numbering them from **1** through **4.**
>
> ______ Joe tried to row to a quarantine station.
> ______ Frisco Kid showed Joe a picture of a family.
> ______ Pete launched the sea anchor.
> ______ The pirates stole an office safe.

These items must be correct in all of their parts for a student's response to be counted correct.

Count spelling errors. Spelling is corrected according to two simple rules.

- If the word appears in the question, it should be spelled correctly in the answer.
- If the word does not appear in the question, it should not be counted wrong if it is misspelled in the answer.

Judge answers to "how" and "why" questions according to the idea they express. Some students do not write appropriate answers to these questions. For example, the item, *Why did she go to the library?* is appropriately answered, "To get a book," or "Because she wanted a book. " Some students, however, may write, "A book." The last answer is unacceptable.

Discussion Questions

Discussion questions are specified after certain lessons. The discussion questions are optional and are intended to give the students a different perspective on the program material.

The discussion questions center on important issues raised by the stories. The teacher presents the question and then asks the students to discuss it. Most of these discussions can be completed within five to ten minutes.

Special Projects

The special projects serve many purposes. They provide a framework for using story information and encourage the use of reference skills. They also encourage student creativity.

The list in the next column shows the special projects and the stories that relate to each project. The students read about each project and choose which one they want to work on.

Lesson Special Projects

23 Drawing pottery designs. (This project relates to the story *The Spider, the Cave and the Pottery Bowl.*)

Making a chart that shows different kinds of ships and boats. (This project relates to the story *The Voyage of the Northern Light.*)

Making up a play based on the last part of *The Odyssey.*

49 Memorizing a poem.

Making a chart that shows the different Greek gods and goddesses. (This project relates to the stories *Persephone* and *The Odyssey.*)

Making up a play based on the last part of *Sara Crewe.*

75 Drawing a picture of the solar system. (This project relates to the story *The Star.*)

Making a scale model of the solar system. (This project relates to the story *The Star.*)

Making a chart that shows the different kinds of large birds. (This project relates to the story *A White Heron.*)

95 Memorizing a poem.

Drawing a map of the United States during the Civil War. (This project relates to the Harriet Tubman biography.)

Making up a play based on the whitewashing incident in *Tom Sawyer.*

115 Writing an ending for *Tom Sawyer.*

Drawing a map of the Mississippi River. (This project relates to the novel *Tom Sawyer.*)

The Management System

The *Reading Mastery VI* management system is simple and effective. It will help you motivate your students, keep track of their progress, and identify the students who need remedial help. The management system has four components.

- The Placement Test
- Remedial Procedures
- The Point System
- The Group Summary Chart

These components are all included in the basic program. There is also an optional *Testing and Management System* (sold separately) which features three other components (mastery tests, an Individual Skills Profile chart, and specific remedial exercises) not found in the basic program.

The Placement Test

The placement test measures the decoding and comprehension skills of students entering *Reading Mastery VI.* You should administer the test, found on page 42, before starting the program. The test results will provide you with:

- information about the reading rate and accuracy of all your students, and information about their ability to answer written comprehension questions
- a means of identifying students who should not be placed in the program, as well as borderline students
- guidelines for grouping your students
- a basis for evaluating student improvement after the students have completed the program

The placement test has two parts. Part 1 of the test is administered individually. Each student reads the passage in Part 1 to you. You time the students and tally their decoding errors. Part 1 requires about two minutes per student.

Part 2 is a group test and is presented to the entire class at the same time. Part 2 requires the students to write answers to comprehension questions about the passage in part 1. Part 2 requires about seven minutes for the entire class.

Instructions for Part 1

Reproduce the Placement Test on page 42 of this guide. Make one copy for each student you are to test. You will need a stopwatch or a clock with a second hand. You should give the test in a place somewhat removed from the other students, so that they will not overhear the testing. Use the following procedures.

1. Give the student a copy of the test.
2. Point to the passage in Part 1 and say, "You're going to read this passage out loud. I want you to read it as well as you can. Don't try to read it so fast that you make mistakes. But don't read it so slowly that it doesn't make any sense. You have two minutes to read the passage. Go."
3. Time the student and tally any errors. Make one tally mark for each error. Count any of the following as one error.
   - misreading a word
   - omitting a word part, for example *s* or *ed* at the end of a word
   - not identifying a word within three seconds
   - sounding out a word but not saying the word at a normal speaking rate
   - skipping a word
   - skipping a line
   - reading a word incorrectly and then reading it correctly
4. Also count each word not read by the end of the two minute time limit as an error. For example, if the student is eight words from the end of the passage at the end of the time limit, count eight errors.
5. Do not correct any errors, with two exceptions.
   - If a student does not identify a word within three seconds, say the word, count it as an error, and then permit the student to continue reading.
   - If a student skips a line, immediately show the student the correct line, and count it as an error.

Instructions for Part 2

Part 2 is administered to the entire group at the same time. After all the students have read the passage in part 1, administer part 2. Use the following procedures.

1. Give each student a copy of the placement test, and make sure the students have pencils.
2. Say, "Here is the passage that you read earlier. Read the passage again silently, and then answer the questions in part 2. You have seven minutes. Go."
3. Collect the test sheets after seven minutes.
4. Total each student's points, using the following answer key.

Answer Key for Part 2

1. King
2. princess
3. *Ideas:* His daughter; Marygold
4. Gold
5. *Idea:* his daughter/gold
6. *Idea:* Because they weren't gold
7. Roses
8. perfume
9. *Idea:* The chink of one coin against another

Placement of Students

Use the following criteria to place the students.

- If a student makes 0 to 6 errors on Part 1 **and** 0 to 2 errors on Part 2, place the student in *Reading Mastery VI.*
- If a student makes more than 6 errors on Part 1 **or** more than 2 errors on Part 2, place the student in *Reading Mastery V*, or use the remedial procedures described on page 40.

You may determine that some students who make more than 6 errors on Part 1 or more than 2 errors on Part 2 are borderline students. Borderline students can enter the program on a trial basis.

Grouping the Students

If the ability level of students in the classroom is fairly similar, *Reading Mastery VI* may be presented to the entire class at once. If the program is too advanced for a small number of students, those students should be placed in another level of *Reading Mastery.* If you identify some of the students as borderline, you may decide to place the advanced students in one group and the borderline students in another group, where they will receive more supervised reading practice. Use the remedial procedures described on page 39 with your borderline students.

Remedial Procedures

The following procedures can be used with students who do not pass the placement test or with borderline students. These procedures may also be used for general remediation at any time during the school year.

Note that the remedial procedures should be kept in perspective. If your schedule does not permit extensive remediation, do not delay teaching the students who qualify for *Reading Mastery VI.* If you have no other choice, place all students in the program and try to provide the students who need help with additional work.

If the students are weak in both decoding and comprehension, work first on decoding.

Decoding Remedies

If the students fail Part 1 of the Placement Test, they are weak in decoding. The simplest remedy for the students who are weak in decoding is to give them practice reading orally. The students should practice oral reading until they are able to read 150 words a minute while making no more than two errors.

Provide the students with stories they can read easily. Set a rate requirement for the students based on the rate at which they can now read, while making no more than two errors per 150 words. As the students improve, change the rate requirement so that they read faster. Continue to give the students practice until they can read at 150 words per minute while making no more than two errors per minute.

Comprehension Remedies

If the students fail part 2 of the Placement Test, they are weak in comprehension. Provide these students with daily practice in answering basic comprehension questions (who, what, when, where, why). Select passages that are easy for the students to read. Call on individual students to read these passages aloud. Ask questions after each sentence is read. Make sure that each question can be clearly answered by the passage that the students are reading. Give the students practice until they are proficient at answering questions.

Readministering the Placement Test

When the students have improved both their comprehension and decoding skills, readminster the Placement Test to those students. If they pass the Placement Test, start them on lesson 1 of *Reading Mastery VI.*

The Daily Point Schedule

The daily point schedule provides an effective system for motivating students and for helping them keep track of their progress. The students earn points for their independent written work, as well as bonus points. Bonus points are given for good oral reading; for completing the writing assignment; for correcting missed items; and for getting all items right. Bonus points also permit you to deal with special problems. Early in the program, you may award bonus points to students who get to their seats on time, who have their material ready for the lesson, or who show in other ways that they are ready to work. Later in the program, you can use bonus points for rewarding good performance. For example, if the students are not paying attention during a particular part of the lesson, announce that there will be a quick test on that part of the lesson. Then give a short oral or written test on that part of the lesson. Students who answer all the questions correctly earn bonus points.

Awarding Points

The students record their points in the boxes that appear at the beginning of each *Workbook* lesson. The students record the points for their independent work in the box labeled **IW**. The students can earn up to eight points for independent work, depending on the number of errors they make. The schedule for awarding points for independent work appears near the end of each lesson in the *Presentation Book.*

The students record bonus points and points for the writing assignment in the box labeled **B**. The students can earn two bonus points for correcting all missed items or for getting all the items right. The students can also earn additional bonus points during the lesson.

In the first ten lessons of the program, the group reads the first part of each story aloud. The group can earn two points for staying within the specified decoding error limit during this reading. The students record these points in the box labeled **R**. Box **R** appears in lessons 1-10 only.

After the students have entered all their points, you total the points and write the total in the box labeled **T**.

The Group Summary Chart

The Group Summary Chart permits you to keep track of the achievement and progress of all your students. Student scores on this chart also provide you with the information you need to assign grades objectively and to diagnose group and individual reading problems. The chart appears on page 43 and may be reproduced for class use.

Keeping a record of your students' achievement on the Group Summary Chart serves several purposes.

You can use the Group Summary Chart as an objective basis for awarding grades. A student who receives ninety percent of the points that can be earned during a grading period earns an **A**. A student who receives eighty to ninety percent of the total earns a **B**, and so forth. This grading system demonstrates to students that grades are not a subjective measure. The students can see how their grades are computed, and can also see that grades are based on daily achievement.

You can use the Group Summary Chart to demonstrate improvement. If the group improves from one week to the next, the Group Summary Chart demonstrates this improvement. Show the chart to the group and praise their achievement.

You can use the Group Summary Chart to diagnose reading problems. The entries you make on the chart show the number of points that each student earns. This information will help you to determine which students need extra help.

Using the Group Summary Chart

To use the chart, you record the number of points that each student earns. You will need to make one copy of the chart for each ten-day span of lessons. Fill in the lesson numbers in the top row of boxes. Begin each new chart with lesson 1, 11, 21, 31, 41, 51, 61, 71, 81, 91, 101, or 111. Fill in student names on the left side of the chart.

After you have completed the workcheck, record individual point totals in each box. After each ten-day span of lessons, total the points in the far right-hand column. Use the points as a basis for assigning grades.

Using Lesson 16 to Diagnose Problems

When you complete lesson 16, your observations of the students during independent work should give you a good idea of whether they are having trouble with particular skill items, with vocabulary items, or with story items.

At lesson 16, be prepared to provide remediation for the more serious problems. The students who are weak in decoding or comprehension should be given remediation before proceeding in the program. Use the remedial procedures discussed on page 39.

If the entire group is weak in decoding, repeat some stories, starting with lesson 12. Note that you don't have to repeat entire lessons, merely the stories.

If the entire group is weak in comprehension, repeat entire lessons, starting with lesson 12. Make sure that all students can correctly answer the comprehension questions. Monitor the students carefully as they do their independent work. Make sure that you have a strong daily workcheck procedure.

If the students are performing well on the first sixteen lessons, they should proceed smoothly through the program. By lesson 16, the students will understand that they are accountable for reading accurately and for understanding what they are reading.

The Optional System

The optional *Testing and Management System* consists of *Test Books* and a *Testing and Management Handbook.* The *Test Books* contain a series of criterion-referenced mastery tests which are administered after every twentieth lesson. Each test item measures student mastery of a specific skill taught in *Reading Mastery VI.* The *Test Books* also include an Individual Skills Profile Chart. The chart lists the skills taught in *Reading Mastery VI* and indicates which test items measure student mastery of those skills. When the chart is completed, it shows how well a student has mastered the skills taught in *Reading Mastery VI.*

Instructions for administering the mastery tests appear in the *Testing and Management Handbooks.* The *Handbooks* also contain remedial exercises for students who do not perform well on the mastery tests. Each test has its own set of remedial exercises, and there is a specific remedial exercise for every tested skill.

Placement Test

Name ______________________________

PART 1

The Golden Touch

Once upon a time there lived a very rich king named Midas, who had a daughter named Marygold.

King Midas was very fond of gold. The only thing he loved more was his daughter. But the more Midas loved his daughter, the more he desired gold. He thought that the best thing he could possibly do for his child would be to give her the largest pile of yellow, glistening coins that had ever been heaped together since the world began. So, Midas gave all his thoughts and all his time to collecting gold. When he gazed at the gold-tinted clouds of sunset, he wished that they were real gold, and that they could be herded into his strong box. When little Marygold ran to meet him with a bunch of buttercups and dandelions, he used to say, "Pooh, pooh, child. If these flowers were as golden as they look, they would be worth picking."

And yet, in his earlier days, before he had this insane desire for gold, King Midas had shown a great love for flowers. He had planted a garden where there were the biggest and sweetest roses that any person ever saw or smelled. These roses were still growing in the garden, as large, as lovely, and as fragrant as they were when Midas used to pass whole hours looking at them, and inhaling their perfume. But now, if he looked at the flowers at all, it was only to calculate how much the garden would be worth if each of the rose petals were a thin plate of gold. And though he once was fond of music, the only music for poor Midas now was the chink of one coin against another.

PART 2

1. *Circle the answer.* What kind of royal person was Midas?

   • Emperor • King • Prince

2. *Circle the answer.* So his daughter was ______.

   • an empress • a queen • a princess

3. What did Midas love most of all?

   ____

4. What did he love almost as much?

   ____

5. But the more Midas loved __________, the more he desired __________.

6. Why didn't Midas think that dandelions were worth picking?

   ____

7. What kind of flowers had Midas planted in his earlier days?

   ____

8. Midas used to inhale the __________ of those flowers.

9. What was the only music that Midas loved now?

   ____

Group Summary Chart

Names	Lessons										Total

Supplementary Novels

Five supplementary novels are recommended for independent student reading after the students have completed lesson 120. The novels, listed in order of difficulty, are:

- *The Black Stallion* - Walter Farley
- *Centerburg Tales* - Robert McCloskey
- *Charlotte's Web* - E.B. White
- *Mrs. Frisby and the Rats of NIMH* - Robert O'Brien
- *Caddie Woodlawn* - Carol Brink

Here are the procedures for introducing the supplementary novels.

Obtain several copies of each novel. All of the novels are widely available through school and public libraries. You can also order the novels from a paperback book club. If you order the novels through a paperback book club, make sure you place your order at least two months before the novels will be needed.

Either assign the novels to individual students or permit the students to select one of the novels. If you assign the novels, you may want to give *The Black Stallion* to below-average students and *Caddie Woodlawn* to above-average students.

Assemble the students who are to read a particular novel. Give them a copy of the word lists and questions for the novel they are to read. (These lists and questions appear on pages 45-56, and they may be reproduced for classroom use.)

Read the word list for section 1 aloud. Each novel has been divided into sections, and each section has its own word lists and questions. Read the word list for section 1 aloud as the students follow along. Then have the students read the word list for section 1. Discuss any words the students do not understand.

Structure the reading of the first two or three pages of the novel. These pages typically contain vocabulary and sentence forms that may be new to the students. Call on individual students to read several sentences in turn. Explain any words or sentences that the students do not understand.

Have the students read the rest of section 1 to themselves. A good procedure is to put a paper clip on the last page of section 1 so that the students know to stop there. After the students finish reading section 1, they must answer the questions for section 1. Correct their answers using the answer keys on pages 57-61.

Follow a similar procedure for each remaining section of the novel. However, the students do not have to read any of the remaining sections aloud.

After the students complete the novel and the questions, direct each student to complete the writing assignment for the novel. You may also want to have the students write a book report on the novel.

The Black Stallion

Section 1 (Chapters 1-5)

Word List

tramp steamer	blunt
prow	eerie
missionary	monotonously
gangplank	turban
tersely	makeshift
accommodation	clambered
inert	stud
bureau	careening
subside	broadside
swerved	grazed
parched	circumference
prone	hypnotize
edible	adjoining
crotch	strove
sustain	venomous
gelatinous	ravine
rhythmic	horsemanship
incredulous	bedlam

Questions

1. At the beginning of the novel, was the stallion wild or tame?
2. Where would the stallion rather be, in a cage or in a field?
3. The stallion came from _____.
   - America
   - India
   - Arabia
4. What happened to the *Drake* during the storm?
5. Who pulled Alec to the island?
6. Alec finally landed on the island. What would have happened to him if he had not been able to cut the rope?
7. Alec struggled to survive on the island.
   a. What food did he find on bushes?
   b. What did he make from driftwood?
   c. Why did he make a spear?
   d. What was the name of the seaweed that Alec ate?
8. On the island, how did the stallion save Alec's life?
9. What happened to Alec the first two times he tried to ride the stallion?
10. How did the stallion change after Alec was able to ride him?
11. What attracted the ship's attention to the island?
12. Why didn't the captain want to take the stallion on the ship?
13. Why did Alec have to fasten a band around the stallion's waist?
14. What happened to Alec's leg?

Section 2 (Chapters 6-9)

Word List

uncanny	instinctive
mingle	supremacy
antiseptic	iron constitution
queasy	spry
clean bill of health	self-reliant
clamored their wares	earmark
yarn	blessing in disguise
beseechingly	rumpus
resignedly	astride
taut	

Questions

1. Which continent is Rio de Janeiro in?
2. Which continent is New York City in?
3. What did Alec buy with the money his parents sent him?
4. When Alec was boarding the ship for New York, why did the stallion break away from him?
5. Why did Alec need to use antiseptic on the stallion?
6. On the ship to New York, why didn't Alec stay in his cabin?
7. What did the stallion do to one of the Quarantine inspectors?
8. Why did Alec have to blindfold the stallion on the New York dock?
9. What was Joe Russo's job?
10. Why was Joe Russo so interested in Alec and the stallion?
11. What kind of building did the stallion live in?
12. Who owned that building?
13. Which other horse lived in that building?
14. What kind of effect did the other horse have on the stallion?
15. What scared the stallion in the middle of the night?
16. Henry thought the stallion would be good at a particular sport. Which sport?
17. What kind of experience did Henry have with that sport?
18. What did the stallion do at the end of this section?

The Black Stallion

Section 3 (Chapters 10-14)

Word List

fairway	gully
staccato	burrs
aroma	sire
dam	registered
pedigree	sheepishly
tutelage	withers
shied	vapor
cinch	contrary
slacken	skittishly
idolized	veteran
jowls	conscientiously
extensive	prophesying
retaliate	charity

Questions

1. Why did Alec think that the stallion would come to the pool?
2. Why didn't Alec tell his mother about the stallion running away?
3. Why did Alec need to get registration papers for the stallion?
4. Why would it be difficult to get those papers?
5. On the first of April, Henry and Alec started training the stallion to _____
6. Which object did they put on the stallion's back?
7. Why didn't the stallion like that object?
8. What kind of place did Henry and Alec take the stallion to at one o'clock in the morning?
9. Why did they bring Napoleon along?
10. Why do you think the stallion loved the track so much?
11. What bad news did the letter bring?
12. Which two horses were going to race in Chicago?
13. Why did Joe Russo think that the stallion could enter that race?
14. Why did Joe Russo want to bring Jim Neville to the track?

Section 4 (Chapters 15-18)

Word List

shindig	brusquely
circulating	foremost authorities
gain momentum	delirious
pulses	faltering
stupendous	temperamental
cocky	streamlined
paddock	plaintively
vantage point	mount
superficial wound	

Questions

1. Was Jim Neville impressed with the stallion?
2. In his column, Jim Neville said that the race in Chicago would no longer prove who was the fastest horse. Why was that?
3. What did the other owners finally agree to do?
4. When Alec told his father about the race, he signalled Henry to come over. Why do you think Alec wanted Henry to talk to his father?
5. What did Alec have to finish before leaving for Chicago?
6. The stallion refused to leave New York unless another animal came with him. Which animal was that?
7. How did Alec and the others get to Chicago?
8. Before the race, how did the other jockeys treat Alec?
9. How did the crowd react when they saw the stallion?
10. What did the stallion do with Sun Raider before the race?
11. What did Sun Raider do to the stallion's leg?
12. Why didn't the stallion start the race with the other horses?
13. In which part of the race did the stallion pass the other horses?
14. Was the stallion's wound serious?
15. Who was the fastest horse in the world?

Writing Assignment

Write a story that explains where the black stallion came from. Make your story at least ten sentences long.

Centerburg Tales

Grandpa Hercules

Word List

nib	monument
commence	axle
contraption	pelts
tread water	putting on airs
feenomina (phenomenon)	peetition (petition)
get your dander up	endorsement
yarn	elaborated
enriched	statistic
disdainfully	knoll

Questions

1. Grampa Herc told a story about a raft trip he took. What did he say stopped his raft in the middle of the creek?
2. Could that really have happened?
3. Explain your answer to question 2.
4. Why did Uncle Ulysses have seventy-two boxes of Whoopsy-Doodles without box tops?
5. Grampa Herc told a story about how he supported a bridge. What did he say happened to the ice he was standing on?
6. So how did he keep standing up?
7. Could that really have happened?
8. Explain your answer to question 7.
9. Grampa Herc told a story about a clock. What did he say was making the clock run slowly?
10. Grampa Herc told a story about panning for gold. In which state was he panning for gold?
11. What made Hopper McThud heavier each time he jumped across the stream?
12. So what happened to Hopper McThud when he took his clothes off?
13. Could that really have happened?
14. Explain your answer to question 13.
15. Mr. Gabby sent Grampa Herc a carton of Gravity-Bitties breakfast food. What was the bottom of each Gravity-Bitty box made out of?
16. According to the directions, you first had to _____ the Gravity-Bitties.
    Then you had to pin the _____ inside your coat.
    Then you had to practice _____.
17. Grampa Herc finally jumped in the middle of March. To which state did he jump?
18. At first, did Uncle Ulysses believe that Grampa Herc had jumped that far?
19. Why did Uncle Ulysses change his mind after he saw the package?
20. Who do you think sent the package?

Experiment 13

Word List

strop	savings bonds
fertilizer	pruned
pollen	subversive
complacent	

Questions

1. What was Dulcy Dooner's uncle famous for?
2. What did Dulcy Dooner inherit from his uncle?
3. Why did everybody think those objects might be valuable?
4. What kind of house did Dulcy plant his seeds in?
5. Why did Homer and Freddy have to knock holes in the roof of that house?
6. At first, how did Dulcy try to make money from the plants?
7. Why did Dulcy's first plan for making money fail?
8. What kinds of plants did Dulcy's plants turn out to be?
9. What fever does that plant give to people?
10. Why did everybody want to leave town?
11. At the meeting, Dulcy made a deal with the town. What would the town pay Dulcy to do?
12. Why couldn't Dulcy keep the money he made from this deal?
13. Homer figured out what would happen if an enemy planted the seeds.
    a. What would everybody in the country be doing after that?
    b. So what would happen to all the activity in the country?
14. The sheriff was going to throw away the seeds in a particular place. Which place?
15. How did Homer get rid of the seeds instead?
16. The number 13 is very important in this story. Name at least three things that involved the number 13.

Centerburg Tales

Eversomuch More So

Word List

awning	exceedingly
elixir	attributable
pompous	instantaneous
unadulterated	texture
sanitary	impurities
metamorphosis	cerebral
led astray	absorbent

Questions

1. What product was Professor Ear selling?
2. According to Professor Ear, when you sprinkled that product on a doughnut, the doughnut tasted _____ delicious.
3. How long was one can of that product supposed to last?
4. The next week, each character was ever so much more like himself.
   a. Which character was ever so much more pompous?
   b. Which character was ever so much more lazy?
   c. Which character was ever so much more uncooperative?
   d. Which character was ever so much more flustered and suspicious?
5. All of those characters felt that Professor Ear had _____ them.
6. Grampa Hercules knew what was really in each can.
   a. How did he feel about that product?
   b. What did he convince the other characters to do?
7. The professor's full name gives you a clue about what EVERSOMUCH MORE-SO really was. The professor's full name was Atmos P.H. Ear.
   a. What word does that name sound like?
   b. So what was in each can?
   c. So Grampa Hercules loved EVERSOMUCH MORE-SO because he loved the _____.
8. According to this story, what are the important things in life?

Pie and Punch and You-Know-Whats

Word List

hypnotize	brandishing
reproachfully	amethyst
tinge	martyr
forte	cadenza
quartet	periodicals
vestibule	septets
predicament	precariously
monotonous	Dewey Decimal System
spasmodic	

Questions

1. At the beginning of the story, what machine kept changing colors?
2. What object did the stranger bring into the lunchroom?
3. The stranger called the boys a "parturient pair of panted Pandoras."
   a. What does "parturient" mean?
   b. Pandora was a woman who let trouble out of a box. So what would a "panted Pandora" be?
   c. In this story, which box does the trouble come out of?
4. What did the boys start doing after they heard the sound?
5. Could the boys control what they were doing?
6. What happened to all the people who heard the boys?
7. Homer knew there was a cure in a story by _____.
8. Which building did all the people go to?
9. Homer finally found the new poem. What happened to him when he told everybody the new poem?
10. Why did everybody tell the new poem to the sixth grade teacher?
11. What would the sixth grade teacher have to do to cure herself?
12. The sheriff played the song on the flip side of the record.
   a. Which animals did that song tell about?
   b. That song gave you the _____.

Writing Assignment

Which story did you like best? Write a paragraph that explains your answer. Make your paragraph at least ten sentences long.

Charlotte's Web

Section 1 (Chapters 1-6)

Word List

a fine specimen
glutton
objectionable
lair
scythes
stealthily
unremitting

Questions

1. At the beginning of the novel, why was Mr. Arable going to kill Wilbur?
2. How did Fern give Wilbur milk?
3. What other kind of person gets milk that way?
4. What is a spring pig?
5. Which family bought Wilbur when he was five weeks old?
6. Which building did Wilbur live in on their place?
7. Name at least three other animals that lived in the building.
8. What would Fern do when she came to that building?
9. One afternoon, what did a goose convince Wilbur to do?
10. Why did the animals' suggestions confuse Wilbur when he was outside?
11. How did Mr. Zuckerman get Wilbur back into the barn?
12. Wilbur made careful plans for the next day. What ruined his plans?
13. Wilbur told the lamb that there couldn't be anything that was less than nothing. Explain how Wilbur reached that conclusion.
14. Wilbur was unhappy because he needed something. What was that?
15. Who offered to be Wilbur's friend?
16. What did Charlotte like to drink?
17. Why was it difficult for Wilbur to like Charlotte at first?
18. What important event happened to the goose?
19. Which object did Templeton roll away?
20. What would that object be like if it broke?

Section 2 (Chapters 7-11)

Word List

detested
anesthetic
buckboards
loathed
conspiracy

Questions

1. The old sheep explained Mr. Zuckerman's plans to Wilbur. What did Mr. Zuckerman plan to do with Wilbur?
2. What did Charlotte say she would do for Wilbur?
3. Why was Mrs. Arable worried about Fern?
4. Mr. Arable said that, "Maybe our ears aren't as sharp as Fern's." What did he mean by that?
5. Wilbur boasted that he could make something that Charlotte made. What was that?
6. How did Wilbur try to make that thing?
7. Were Wilbur's efforts successful?
8. How did Wilbur feel about life and the world?
9. What did Avery try to do to Charlotte?
10. Why was there such a rotten smell in the air after Avery did that?
11. How did the smell save Charlotte's life?
12. The next morning, which two words did Charlotte write in her web?
13. Why did the people think that was a miracle?
14. Why did everybody come to the Zuckerman's farm?
15. Why did Fern think that the barn was less pleasant now?

Charlotte's Web

Section 3 (Chapters 12-17)

Word List

baser instincts	destiny
adjourn	rummaging
incessant	reputation
forsake	veritable treasure
yarn	surpass
stowaway	pummel
lacerated	listless

Questions

1. At the meeting, Charlotte explained why she had written the words in her web. Why had she written them?
2. Why wouldn't Mr. Zuckerman want to kill Wilbur now?
3. Why did Charlotte want to write a new word?
4. What did Charlotte want Templeton to get for her?
5. How did Templeton depend upon Wilbur?
6. What was the next word that Charlotte wrote?
7. Which event did Mr. Zuckerman decide to take Wilbur to?
8. Where did the words "with new radiant action" come from?
9. Charlotte told Wilbur a story about a cousin of hers and a fish. What happened in the story?
10. Why did Mrs. Arable go to visit Dr. Dorian?
11. What did Dr. Dorian think the real miracle was?
12. Dr. Dorian thought there was a reason that he had never heard animals talking. What was the reason?
13. What was the next word that Charlotte wrote in her web?
14. What did the crickets sing about?
15. Why did Charlotte need to build a sac?
16. What kind of bath did Mrs. Zuckerman give Wilbur?
17. How did the sheep convince Templeton to go to the fair?
18. What did Mr. Arable say that made Wilbur faint?
19. At the fair, what was the pig next to Wilbur like?
20. Why did Charlotte think that pig would be hard for Wilbur to beat?
21. How did Charlotte plan to help Wilbur?

Section 4 (Chapters 18-22)

Word List

schemer	carousing
gorge	confetti
sentiments	hallowed

Questions

1. Why was Mrs. Arable so happy when she saw Fern in the Ferris wheel?
2. What was the last word that Charlotte made in her web?
3. What other object did Charlotte make?
4. Why wouldn't Charlotte ever see her children?
5. Which pig won first prize?
6. What kind of prize did Wilbur win?
7. After Wilbur won the prize, who was Fern more interested in?
8. What made Wilbur faint again?
9. What was the greatest moment in Mr. Zuckerman's life?
10. What did Charlotte tell Wilbur that made him cry?
11. What did Wilbur want Templeton to get for him?
12. What deal did Wilbur make with Templeton?
13. How did Wilbur carry the egg sac back home?
14. What happened to Charlotte after Wilbur left?
15. Why did Wilbur know that Mr. Zuckerman would keep him for as long as he lived?
16. What happened to Templeton because of his deal with Wilbur?
17. What came out of Charlotte's sac one day?
18. How did most of the spiders leave the barn?
19. How many spiders stayed in the barn?
20. How did Fern change?
21. How did Wilbur feel about the barn?
22. Charlotte was in a class by herself because she had two important qualities. Name those two qualities.

Writing Assignment

The people in the book thought that Charlotte's writing was a miracle. Do you believe that there are miracles? Write a paragraph that explains your answer. Make your paragraph at least ten sentences long.

Mrs. Frisby and the Rats of NIMH

Section 1 (Chapters 1-7)

Word List

cinder block
texture
filtering
fare
warily
parsnip
corn shuck
authoritatively
pallet
roundabout
botanically
prospect
cocoon
eaves
idling
plummet
primeval
sonorous
access
rancid
depressed
sward
furrowed
protrude
lath
hypochondriac
relentlessly
hermit
delirious
capacity
harrow
reputation
essence
expedition
slither
dietary

Questions

1. What kind of object did Mrs. Frisby and her family live in?
2. What kind of garden was that object in?
3. Why didn't Timothy join his family for breakfast?
4. Why did Mrs. Frisby go to see Mr. Ages?
5. Why did Mrs. Frisby take such a roundabout way to Mr. Ages' house?
6. What kinds of things did Mr. Ages collect in his sack?
7. What disease did Timothy have?
8. What problem did the crow have?
9. How did Mrs. Frisby free the crow?
10. How did the crow help Mrs. Frisby in return?
11. Why would the Frisby family have to move out of the garden?
12. What might happen to Timothy if the Frisby family moved?
13. Mrs. Frisby found out about Mr. Fitzgibbon's plans. How many days did she have left to move her family?
14. When Mrs. Frisby was coming home, the cat did something unusual. What was that?
15. Mrs. Frisby saw some rats. What were they doing?
16. Where did the crow take Mrs. Frisby at dusk one evening?
17. Describe what the owl's home was like.

Section 2 (Chapters 8-14)

Word List

deference
lamely
domain
intertwined
hostile
laboriously
pry
recounted
contritely
conceivably
prowl
trespassers
rarity
urgent
explicit
incomprehensible
baffled
entranced

Questions

1. The owl became very interested in Mrs. Frisby after she told him something. What did she tell him?
2. What did the owl think that the rats could do with Mrs. Frisby's house?
3. What is the lee side of a barn?
4. What sort of bush did the rats live under?
5. What was Brutus guarding?
6. Why did Mrs. Frisby begin to leave the rosebush?
7. Why was Mrs. Frisby able to see when they were far under ground?
8. What did Mrs. Frisby and the others take instead of the stairs?
9. In what kind of room did Mrs. Frisby wait for the others?
10. What did Mrs. Frisby think was so unusual about the rats?
11. Why did Mrs. Frisby know how to read?
12. Nicodemus figured out what the lee side of the stone was. What was it?
13. How did the rats usually protect themselves from the cat?
14. What task did Mrs. Frisby volunteer to do?
15. What had happened to Mr. Frisby when he had done that?
16. Describe what Nicodemus's room was like.
17. Where had Nicodemus grown up?
18. Where did he get food from?
19. What did the people from the NIMH truck do to Nicodemus one night?

Mrs. Frisby and the Rats of NIMH

Section 3 (Chapters 15-21)

Word List

inextricably
futile
scientifically compiled
biologist
illusion
wryly
dictated
unerringly
ritual
foresee
plaintive
pry open
cursory
primarily
portal
case the place
undergo
injection
maze
at large
underestimating
inkling
undoing
astute
shafts
consternation
roving
satchel
debated

Questions

1. What kind of place were Nicodemus and the other rats taken to?
2. What were Dr. Schultz and the others doing with the rats?
3. How did Dr. Schultz put liquid into the rats?
4. What was the first kind of test that Nicodemus took?
5. What did that test tell Dr. Schultz about the rats?
6. What did Justin try to do one day?
7. How was the A group different from the other two groups?
8. What had made them so different?
9. Which other group of animals was like the A group of rats?
10. What did Dr. Schultz teach the rats to do with words?
11. Why did Justin know how to open his cage?
12. What passageway did Justin discover behind the baseboard?
13. Where did that passageway lead?
14. Why did the rats use string when they explored the passageway?
15. What happened to six of the mice in the passageway?
16. How did the other two mice help the rats escape?
17. How did the rats learn while they were at the Boniface Estate?
18. What kinds of things did Mrs. Frisby see in the main hall?
19. What were the rats going to use the plow for?
20. For the Plan, the rats would live without _____.
21. After they left the Boniface Estate, the rats decide to live _____the ground.
22. Which dead person did the rats find?

Mrs. Frisby and the Rats of NIMH

Section 4 (Chapters 22-28)

Word List

precautions
cynical
irrigation
denounce
colander
insulation
federal government
cyanide
exert
commence
pulleys
cryptically
flexed
stubble
exterminate
pessimist
drought
admonish
electrocuted
short circuit
epidemic
deposit
impasse
hillock
precision
dispatch
cleated
incredulously

Questions

1. What useful things did the rats find in the Toy Tinker's truck?
2. How did the rats get electricity for their cave?
3. Why did the rats become discontented with their life?
4. Why did the rats fear Mr. Fitzgibbon?
5. One day, Nicodemus took Jenner to a place in the woods. What was the name of that place?
6. Why was Nicodemus interested in that place?
7. Why didn't Jenner agree with Nicodemus's plan?
8. Why did Jenner leave the other rats?
9. Why did Mrs. Frisby go to the cat's bowl?
10. What did Bill Fitzgibbon do to Mrs. Frisby after she did that?
11. Mrs. Frisby found out what had happened to the other rats.
    a. What were they trying to take from the hardware store?
    b. What killed them?
    c. Why was the government so interested in those rats?
    d. What was the government going to do for Mr. Fitzgibbon?
12. Who rescued Mrs. Frisby from the bird cage?
13. What did the rats do for Mrs. Frisby after she escaped from the birdcage?
14. Why did the rats destroy their home before they left it?
15. Why did ten of the rats stay behind?
16. Before some of those rats escaped into the woods, they ran around in circles. Why did they do that?
17. Where did Mrs. Frisby and her family move to later that year?
18. Where were they thinking about moving at the end of the novel?

Writing Assignment

Do you think that animals could be as smart as people? Write a paragraph that explains your answer. Make your paragraph at least ten sentences long.

Caddie Woodlawn

Section 1 (Chapters 1-6)

Word List

inseparable
massacre
virtues
relenting
calico
sheaths
unpardonable
sedate
cameo brooch
escapade
victuals
christening
irksome
unfathomable
abolition
reproachfully
wholesale slaughter
moderation
sheepishly
ruefully
reverberated
deft
bribe
salvage
pompously
loons
fowl
seamstress
denim
muffler
pommeling
pioneer
scalp belt
irresolutely
pitch
pliable
venison
disheveled
fervor
sampler
incite
enthrall
benediction
pendulum
genial
aristocrats
vibrant
glutton
Cheshire cat
ominously
fife and drum corps
treading
inefficient
infamy
silhouetted
wheedle
enterprise
barbarous
billows
challis
clannish
admonish

Questions

1. Did Caddie act like the other girls in her family?
2. Which family members did Caddie play with and act like?
3. Who wanted Caddie to run wild, her mother or her father?
4. Which Indian was friendly with Caddie?
5. What did the Circuit Rider do for a living?
6. What did Caddie do to disgrace herself when she met the Circuit Rider?
7. What did the Circuit Rider ask Mr. Woodlawn to repair?
8. Which birds did all the people hunt?
9. The writer compared those birds to a group of people who were fighting a losing battle with the white people. Which people were like the birds?
10. What was Uncle Edmund always doing to people?
11. What did Uncle Edmund do to Caddie's raft?
12. Why did Uncle Edmund give Caddie a silver dollar?
13. Why did Uncle Edmund take Nero with him?
14. During which season did school begin?
15. Why didn't school go on all year round?
16. What did the teacher do to Obediah Jones in front of the class?
17. How did Obediah treat the teacher after that incident?

Caddie Woodlawn

Section 2 (Chapters 7-12)

Word List

tumultuous
rivalry
compartments
accumulate
clogs
murals
thrifty
beau
elation
in her element
smelling salts
pored over
exasperation
draughty
breeches
hassocks
pursed his lips
miserly
indolent
inconsolable
boastful

Questions

1. What happened to Caddie when she went skating on thin ice?
2. Why did Caddie have to stay inside for most of the winter?
3. What skill did Caddie learn from her father that winter?
4. Was Mr. Woodlawn's English family royal or ordinary?
5. Why was Mr. Woodlawn's father ordered to leave that family?
6. What did Mr. Woodlawn do to earn money for his mother and father?
7. Why do you think that Mr. Woodlawn did not want to go back to England?
8. What deal did the Woodlawn children make with the Hankinson children?
9. Why were the Woodlawn children so happy with that deal?
10. What bad news was in Uncle Edmund's letter?
11. What rumor did Mr. Kent bring to the Woodlawns?
12. Why did all the neighbors gather at the Woodlawn's house?
13. Caddie overheard some men talking about the Indians. What did those men want to do to the Indians?
14. Why did Caddie go see Indian John?
15. What did the Indians plan to do the next day?
16. Who met Caddie on her way back home?
17. What did Mr. Woodlawn and John agree to do?

Section 3 (Chapters 13-18)

Word List

portage
confirmation
meter
inadvertently
conspicuously
furrows
good riddance
incredulously
partridge
arbutus
bunting
foreboding
novelty

Questions

1. Why were the Indians moving westward for a time?
2. Which two presents did Indian John give Caddie?
3. How did the children plan to make money from the scalp belt?
4. Why did Mrs. Hankinson have to leave town?
5. What did Caddie do with her silver dollar?
6. Even though she didn't buy anything for herself, Caddie felt she'd gotten her dollar's worth. Why?
7. What did Robert Ireton do to entertain the children?
8. Why had Katie Hyman become sick?
9. Why was Tom so embarrassed when his eyes met Katie's?
10. What did the students have to perform on "speaking" day?
11. What was wrong with Warren's performance?
12. During the storm, what happened to the oak tree right after the children left it?
13. Tom told the story of Pee Wee.
    a. What did Pee Wee end up getting for his dead oxen?
    b. What did Pee Wee end up getting for his dead wife?
    c. Why did Pee Wee get all the farmers' land?
14. Why was Hetty so happy to be with Caddie?
15. What terrible news did the Circuit Rider bring?

Caddie Woodlawn

Section 4 (Chapters 19-24)

Word List

churning	apparition
city airs	pandemonium
conviction	stupendous
culprits	remorse
plaintive	tremulously

Questions

1. What kind of language did Annabelle use in her letter?
2. What did Indian John's dog warn the school about?
3. How did Obediah and the other boys keep the fire away from the school?
4. Annabelle wanted to be as un_____ as the Woodlawn children.
5. What did the sheep do to Annabelle as she held the salt?
6. What trick did Caddie play on Annabelle in the hayloft?
7. Why was Caddie singled out for punishment?
8. What was Caddie planning to do before her father came to see her?
9. Caddie's father thought that women should teach men certain ways to behave. Name some of those ways.
10. What news did the letter from England bring?
11. What kinds of things would the family gain if they moved to England?
12. What kinds of things would the family have to give up if they moved to England?
13. How did the family decide what to do?
14. Why do you think they decided to stay?
15. Which traveler came home at the end of the novel?
16. The last sentence of the novel says that Caddie Woodlawn was a _____ and an _____.

Writing Assignment

Caddie Woodlawn and Tom Sawyer are alike in many ways, and different in other ways. Write a paragraph that compares Caddie Woodlawn and Tom Sawyer. Make your paragraph at least ten sentences long.

Answer Key

The Black Stallion

Section 1

1. Wild
2. In a field
3. Arabia
4. *Idea:* It sank
5. *Idea:* The stallion
6. *Idea:* He would have been dragged across the beach
7. a. *Idea:* Berries
   b. *Idea:* A shelter
   c. *Idea:* To catch fish
   d. Carragheen
8. *Idea:* By killing a snake
9. *Idea:* He was thrown off
10. *Ideas:* He was tamer; he took orders
11. *Idea:* The fire.
12. *Ideas:* He was too wild; they couldn't handle him
13. *Idea:* So he could be lifted on to the ship
14. *Idea:* The stallion kicked it

Section 2

1. South America
2. North America
3. *Idea:* Tickets to New York for the stallion and himself
4. *Idea:* To fight the chestnut stallion
5. *Idea:* Because he had been cut in the fight
6. *Idea:* Because he stayed with the stallion
7. *Idea:* Knocked him over
8. *Idea:* So he wouldn't be frightened
9. *Idea:* Reporter
10. *Idea:* They were a good story for the newspaper
11. A barn
12. *Idea:* The Daileys
13. Napoleon
14. *Idea:* He calmed him down
15. *Idea:* Tony
16. *Idea:* Horse racing
17. *Idea:* He had been a jockey
18. *Idea:* Ran away

Section 3

1. *Idea:* To get water
2. *Ideas:* It would worry her; she might make him give up the stallion
3. *Idea:* So that the stallion could enter races
4. *Ideas:* Because the former owner had drowned; because Alec didn't know where the horse was from
5. race
6. A saddle
7. *Ideas:* It was heavy; it hampered him
8. *Idea:* A race track
9. *Idea:* To calm down the stallion
10. *Ideas:* Because he could run; because it made him feel free
11. *Idea:* The stallion wasn't registered
12. Cyclone and Sun Raider
13. *Ideas:* Because it was a special race; because the horses didn't need to be registered
14. *Idea:* To show him the stallion

Section 4

1. Yes
2. *Idea:* Because the stallion was faster
3. *Idea:* Let the stallion into the race
4. *Idea:* So he could convince him to let Alec race
5. *Idea:* His exams
6. Napoleon
7. *Idea:* On a train
8. *Idea:* They made fun of him
9. *Idea:* They were impressed
10. *Idea:* Got into a fight
11. *Ideas:* Hit it; made it bleed
12. *Idea:* Because Alec was looking at his leg
13. *Idea:* At the end
14. No
15. *Idea:* The stallion

Answer Key

Centerburg Tales

Grandpa Hercules

1. *Idea:* A bump in the creek
2. No
3. *Idea:* A creek can't have a bump in it
4. *Idea:* Because the children had used the box tops to get balls and tops
5. *Idea:* It cracked
6. *Idea:* By treading water
7. No
8. *Idea:* A person can't stand on water
9. *Idea:* The weight of the sparrows
10. California
11. *Idea:* He was carrying more gold each time
12. *Idea:* He hopped very far
13. No
14. *Idea:* A person can't hop that far
15. Lead
16. eat/bottom/jumping
17. Indiana
18. No
19. *Idea:* Because the package contained Grampa Herc's clothes
20. *Idea:* The children

Experiment 13

1. *Idea:* Breeding seeds
2. *Idea:* Seeds
3. *Idea:* They might turn into valuable plants
4. *Idea:* A greenhouse
5. *Idea:* To let the plants through
6. *Idea:* By charging people to look at them
7. *Idea:* Because people could see the plants from everywhere
8. Ragweed
9. Hay fever
10. *Idea:* They didn't want to get hay fever
11. *Idea:* Stop growing ragweeds
12. *Idea:* Because the town made a tax on ragweed seeds
13. a. *Idea:* Sneezing
    b. *Idea:* It would stop
14. *Idea:* The ocean
15. *Idea:* By baking them into the doughnuts
16. *Ideas:* The experiment number; the number of seeds Dulcy planted; Dulcy's bill; the number of doughnuts Homer made

Eversomuch More-So

1. EVERSOMUCH MORE-SO
2. ever so much more so
3. *Idea:* A lifetime
4. a. The Judge
   b. Uncle Ulysses
   c. Dulcy Dooner
   d. The Sheriff
5. swindled
6. a. *Idea:* He loved it
   b. *Idea:* Keep their cans
7. a. Atmosphere
   b. *Ideas:* Atmosphere; air
   c. *Ideas:* atmosphere; air
8. *Ideas:* Atmosphere; air; green grass; birds singing; water

Pie and Punch and You-Know-Whats

1. The jukebox
2. A record
3. a. *Idea:* Just about to let something out
   b. *Idea:* A man who lets trouble out of a box
   c. The jukebox
4. *Idea:* Singing
5. No
6. *Idea:* They started singing
7. Mark Twain
8. *Idea:* The library
9. *Idea:* He stopped singing
10. *Idea:* So they could stop saying it
11. *Idea:* Tell the poem to someone else
12. a. Hippopotamuses
    b. hiccups

Answer Key

Charlotte's Web

Section 1

1. *Idea:* Because Wilbur was a runt
2. *Idea:* From a bottle
3. A baby
4. *Idea:* A pig born in the spring
5. The Zuckermans
6. The barn
7. *Ideas:* Sheep; geese; rats; spiders; cows; horses
8. *Idea:* Watch Wilbur
9. *Idea:* Escape
10. *Idea:* Because they all told him something different to do
11. *Idea:* He gave him a pail of food
12. Rain
13. *Idea:* Because nothing is the lowest you can go
14. *Ideas:* A friend; love
15. Charlotte
16. Blood
17. *Idea:* Because she was so bloodthirsty and violent
18. *Idea:* Her eggs hatched
19. *Idea:* One of the eggs
20. *Ideas:* Smelly; rotten

Section 2

1. *Idea:* Kill him
2. *Idea:* Save him
3. *Idea:* Because she heard the animals talking
4. *Idea:* That grownups can't hear the same things children can
5. A web
6. *Idea:* By tying a string to his tail and jumping off the pile
7. No
8. *Idea:* He loved it
9. *Idea:* Kill her
10. *Idea:* Because Avery broke the egg
11. *Idea:* Because Avery ran away
12. Some Pig
13. *Idea:* Because spiders can't write
14. *Idea:* To see Wilbur
15. *Idea:* There were too many people

Section 3

1. *Idea:* To save Wilbur's life
2. *Idea:* Because he thought Wilbur was an unusual pig
3. *Idea:* Because people were getting bored of the old words
4. *Idea:* Words from magazines
5. *Idea:* He ate his food
6. Terrific
7. The fair
8. *Idea:* From a package of soap flakes
9. *Idea:* The spider caught the fish and ate it
10. *Idea:* Because she was worried about Fern
11. *Idea:* That a spider could make a web
12. *Idea:* That he hadn't been paying attention
13. Radiant
14. *Idea:* The end of summer
15. *Idea:* To lay eggs
16. *Idea:* A buttermilk bath
17. *Idea:* By telling him about all the food there
18. *Idea:* That they were still going to kill him
19. *Idea:* Big
20. *Idea:* Because he was so big
21. *Idea:* By spinning another web

Section 4

1. *Idea:* Because Fern was with Henry Fussy
2. Humble
3. *Idea:* Her egg sac
4. *Idea:* Because she would die
5. Uncle
6. *Idea:* A special award
7. Henry Fussy
8. *Idea:* The cheering of the crowd
9. *Idea:* When he received the prize for Wilbur
10. *Idea:* That she was going to die
11. *Idea:* Charlotte's egg sac
12. *Idea:* That Templeton could eat his food first
13. *Idea:* In his mouth
14. *Idea:* She died
15. *Idea:* Because he had won the prize
16. *Idea:* He got very fat
17. *Idea:* Little spiders
18. *Idea:* By making little balloons and floating away
19. 3
20. *Idea:* She didn't come to the barn any more
21. *Idea:* He loved it
22. *Idea:* She was a true friend; she was a good writer

Answer Key

Mrs. Frisby and the Rats of NIMH

Section 1

1. *Idea:* A cinder block
2. *Idea:* A vegetable garden
3. *Idea:* He was sick
4. *Idea:* To get medicine for Timothy
5. *Idea:* Because she was afraid of the cat
6. *Idea:* Plants
7. Pneumonia
8. *Idea:* He was tied to the fence with string
9. *Idea:* She bit through the string
10. *Idea:* Gave her a ride home
11. *Idea:* Because the farmer was going to plow it
12. *Idea:* He might die
13. 5
14. *Ideas:* It didn't chase her; it stayed asleep
15. *Idea:* Carrying a cable
16. *Idea:* To the owl's house
17. *Idea:* A hole in a tree

Section 2

1. *Idea:* Her name
2. *Idea:* Move it to a safe place
3. *Idea:* The side where the wind doesn't blow
4. *Idea:* A rosebush
5. *Idea:* A tunnel entrance
6. *Idea:* Because Brutus wouldn't let her in
7. *Idea:* Because the tunnel had electric lights
8. An elevator
9. A library
10. *Idea:* The rats were living like people
11. *Idea:* Her husband had taught her
12. *Idea:* The part where the farmer didn't plow
13. *Idea:* By giving him sleeping powder
14. *Idea:* Give the powder to the cat
15. *Idea:* The cat had killed him
16. *Ideas:* Rug; bookshelves; sofa; radio
17. *Idea:* In a city
18. *Idea:* A market
19. *Idea:* Captured him

Section 3

1. *Idea:* A laboratory
2. *Idea:* Conducting an experiment
3. *Idea:* By injection
4. *Idea:* Running a maze
5. *Idea:* How quickly they learned
6. *Idea:* Escape
7. *Ideas:* They were smarter; they didn't age as quickly
8. *Idea:* The injections
9. *Idea:* The G group of mice
10. *Idea:* Read
11. *Idea:* He read the instructions
12. *Idea:* The air ducts
13. *Idea:* To the outside
14. *Idea:* So they wouldn't get lost
15. *Idea:* They were blown away
16. *Idea:* They crawled through the screen and pulled back the bolt
17. *Idea:* By reading the books
18. *Ideas:* Rats working with tools; rats hauling things
19. *Idea:* To plant crops
20. stealing
21. under
22. The Toy Tinker

Section 4

1. *Ideas:* Tools; motors
2. *Idea:* By tapping Mr. Fitzgibbon's power line
3. *Idea:* Because they had to steal
4. *Idea:* Because he might discover them
5. Thorn Valley
6. *Idea:* He thought the rats could move there
7. *Idea:* He thought the rats could live off people
8. *Idea:* Because he was opposed to the Plan
9. *Idea:* To put sleeping powder in
10. *Idea:* Caught her
11. a. A motor
    b. Electricity
    c. *Idea:* Because they were the rats from the experiment
    d. *Idea:* Get rid of the rats
12. Justin
13. *Idea:* Moved her house
14. *Idea:* So the people wouldn't suspect anything
15. *Idea:* So the people would see them leaving
16. *Idea:* So the people would think there were many of them
17. *Idea:* To the field
18. *Idea:* To Thorn Valley

Answer Key

Caddie Woodlawn

Section 1

1. No
2. *Idea:* Her brothers
3. Her father
4. Indian John
5. *Idea:* Traveled and held services
6. *Idea:* Spilled nuts all over the floor
7. His clock
8. Passenger pigeons
9. *Idea:* The Indians
10. *Idea:* Playing jokes on them
11. *Idea:* Took it apart
12. *Ideas:* To make up for his joke; so she would forgive him
13. *Idea:* To turn him into a hunting dog
14. Winter
15. *Idea:* Because there was only one teacher
16. *Idea:* Hit him with a ruler
17. *Idea:* He obeyed her

Section 2

1. *Idea:* She fell into the water
2. *Idea:* Because she got sick
3. *Idea:* Repairing clocks
4. Royal
5. *Idea:* He married a common woman
6. *Idea:* Danced
7. *Idea:* Because England had mistreated his family
8. *Idea:* They traded lunches
9. *Idea:* They were sick of turkey
10. *Idea:* Nero had run away.
11. *Idea:* That the Indians were going to attack
12. *Idea:* To prepare for the Indians
13. *Idea:* Kill them
14. *Idea:* To warn them
15. *Idea:* Leave
16. *Idea:* Mr. Woodlawn
17. *Idea:* Keep the peace

Section 3

1. *Ideas:* Because of the massacre scare; because the whites mistrusted them
2. *Idea:* The dog and the scalp belt
3. *Idea:* By charging people to look at it
4. *Idea:* Because she was Indian
5. *Idea:* Bought presents for the Hankinson children
6. *Idea:* Because she'd made the children happy
7. *Idea:* Sang a song
8. *Idea:* Because she had been frightened by what might happen to Caddie
9. *Idea:* Because he had sent her the valentine
10. *Idea:* Songs and poems
11. *Idea:* He couldn't remember the words of his poem
12. *Idea:* It was struck by lightning
13. a. Money
    b. *Idea:* A coach and horses
    c. *Idea:* He convinced all the farmers to jump in the lake
14. *Idea:* Because no one played with her
15. *Idea:* That Lincoln had been shot

Section 4

1. *Idea:* Very proper and correct
2. A fire
3. *Idea:* By digging trenches and beating down the grass
4. civilized
5. *Idea:* Climbed all over her
6. *Idea:* Slipped an egg down her back
7. *Idea:* Because she was a girl
8. *Idea:* Run away
9. *Ideas:* Gentleness; courtesy; love; kindness
10. *Idea:* That Mr. Woodlawn had inherited a lot of money
11. *Ideas:* Money; royalty; power
12. *Ideas:* Their farm; their friends; their freedom
13. *Idea:* By voting
14. *Idea:* Because they were so happy
15. Nero
16. pioneer/American

Scope and Sequence Chart

The following scope and sequence chart provides an overview of the skills taught in *Reading Mastery VI.* The skills are divided into four principal areas: comprehension skills, decoding skills, literary skills, and study skills.

The numbers on the chart indicate which lessons offer practice in a given skill. When a span of lessons is shown in regular type (1-20, for example), **every** lesson in the span offers practice in the skill. When a span of lessons is shown in italic type (*1-20*, for example), **most** lessons in the span offer practice in the skill.

Decoding Skills

Words

- Reading regularly spelled words: 1-120
- Reading irregularly spelled words: 1-120

Sentences and Stories

- Reading aloud: 1-120
- Reading silently: 1-120

Comprehension Skills

Comprehension Readiness

- Following oral directions: 1-120

Vocabulary

- Identifying the meanings of common words and phrases: *1-120*
- Comprehending vocabulary definitions: 1-120
- Using vocabulary words in context: 1-120
- Completing crossword puzzles: 21, 28, 36, 51, 60, 71, 81, 91, 120
- Using context to predict word meaning: 3-120

Literal Comprehension

- Answering literal questions about a text: 1-120
- Identifying literal causes and effects: *1-120*
- Recalling details and events: 1-120
- Following written directions: 1-120
- Sequencing narrative events: *1-120*

Interpretive Comprehension

- Predicting narrative outcomes: *1-120*
- Inferring causes and effects: *1-120*
- Inferring story details and events: *1-120*
- Making comparisons: *1-120*
- Inferring main idea: 15-20, 23, 24, 27, 28, 32, 35, 41, 49, 64
- Inferring details relevant to main idea: 15-28, 30, 31, 34, 38, 46, 58, 69
- Outlining: 80-84, 116, 120

Reasoning

- Drawing conclusions: *1-120*
- Evaluating problems and solutions: *1-120*
- Distinguishing between relevant and irrelevant evidence: 21-31, 33, 37, 42,
- Identifying contradictions: 32-42, 45, 65, 72, 85, 106
- Completing written deductions: 54-59, 61-64, 97
- Distinguishing between literal and inferential questions: 56-60, 63, 66, 68
- Identifying logical fallacies: 94-120

Literary Skills

Analyzing Characters and Settings

- Interpreting a character's feelings: *1-120*
- Pretending to be a character: *1-120*
- Interpreting a character's motives: *1-120*
- Inferring a character's point of view: *1-120*
- Predicting a character's actions: *1-120*
- Identifying features of a setting: *1-120*
- Identifying a character's traits: *1-120*

Literary Devices

- Interpreting similes: 39-44, 46-50, 53, 57-60, 62, 70, 72, 78, 84, 96
- Interpreting exaggeration: 45-48, 55, 57-60, 69, 88, 108
- Interpreting metaphors: 49-60, 67, 77, 107
- Interpreting sarcasm: 59-62, 71, 88
- Interpreting extended dialogues: 61-67, 79, 110
- Interpreting substitute words: 66-68, 71-75, 101
- Interpreting shortened sentences: 69-73, 89
- Interpreting combined sentences: 74-83, 86, 91, 104
- Interpreting irony: 88-92, 96, 102, 111

Types of Literature

- Reading realistic fiction: *1-120*
- Reading fantasy: 5-13, 29-34, 73-75
- Reading short stories: 1-3, 14-34, 50-57, 73-75
- Reading novels: 5-13, 36-49, 59-70, 91-120
- Reading biographies: 76-82
- Reading poetry: 35, 36, 58, 59, 71-73, 86, 87
- Reading plays: 83-85

Study Skills

Writing

- Writing answers to questions: 1-120
- Completing writing assignments: 1-120

Using Reference Materials

- Reading informational passages: 1, 4, 21, 24, 27, 36, 56, 60, 71, 73, 76, 8
- Interpreting maps: 4-13, 15, 17, 18, 21, 23, 24, 27, 33, 40, 63, 67, 68, 70
- Filling out forms: 81-84, 87, 103, 114
- Identifying proper reference sources: 85-90, 94
- Interpreting graphs: 92-97, 100, 101, 105, 115

Behavioral Objectives

The following chart gives specific objectives for each skill taught in *Reading Mastery VI.* Three columns of information are provided. The **Behavioral objective** column details the kind of performance that can be expected from a student who has mastered the skill. The column headed **The student is asked to** describes the tasks the student performs in order to master the skill. The **Lessons** column shows the lessons in which the skill appears. Lesson numbers shown in regular type indicate that **every** lesson provides practice in this skill; numbers in italic type indicate that **most** lessons provide practice in this skill.

DECODING SKILLS: WORDS

READING REGULARLY SPELLED WORDS

Behavioral objective	The student is asked to	Lessons
When presented with a list of regularly spelled words, the student is able to read the list without error.	Orally read lists of regularly spelled words.	1-120

READING IRREGULARLY SPELLED WORDS

Behavioral objective	The student is asked to	Lessons
When presented with a list of irregularly spelled words, the student is able to read the list without error.	Orally read lists of irregularly spelled words.	1-120

DECODING SKILLS: SENTENCES AND STORIES

READING ALOUD

Behavioral objective	The student is asked to	Lessons
When presented with a reading selection, the student is able to read the selection aloud with a minimum of decoding errors.	Read part of a *Textbook* selection aloud.	1-120

READING SILENTLY

Behavioral objective	The student is asked to	Lessons
When presented with a reading selection, the student is able to read the selection silently.	Read part of a *Textbook* selection silently.	1-120

COMPREHENSION SKILLS: COMPREHENSION READINESS

FOLLOWING ORAL DIRECTIONS

Behavioral objective	The student is asked to	Lessons
When given oral directions, the student is able to follow them.	Follow directions presented orally by the teacher.	1-120

COMPREHENSION SKILLS: VOCABULARY

IDENTIFYING THE MEANINGS OF COMMON WORDS AND PHRASES

Behavioral objective	The student is asked to	Lessons
When presented with a common word or phrase, the student is able to explain what it means.	Explain the meaning of a common word or phrase used in a *Textbook* selection.	*1-120*

COMPREHENDING VOCABULARY DEFINITIONS

Behavioral objective	The student is asked to	Lessons
When presented with a written definition of a vocabulary word, the student is able to comprehend the definition.	Explain the meaning of a defined vocabulary word.	1-120

USING VOCABULARY WORDS IN CONTEXT

Behavioral objective	The student is asked to	Lessons
When presented with a vocabulary word, the student is able to use the word correctly within a sentence.	Use a vocabulary word correctly within a sentence.	1-120

COMPLETING CROSSWORD PUZZLES

Behavioral objective	The student is asked to	Lessons
When presented with a crossword puzzle employing vocabulary words, the student is able to complete the puzzle.	Use vocabulary words to complete a crossword puzzle.	21, 28, 36, 51, 60, 71, 81, 91, 120

USING CONTEXT TO PREDICT WORD MEANING

Behavioral objective	The student is asked to	Lessons
When presented with a sentence containing a vocabulary word, the student is able to use context to predict the meaning of the vocabulary word.	Use sentence context to predict the meaning of a vocabulary word.	3-120

COMPREHENSION SKILLS: LITERAL COMPREHENSION

ANSWERING LITERAL QUESTIONS ABOUT A TEXT

Behavioral objective	The student is asked to	Lessons
When presented with literal questions about a reading selection, the student is able to answer the questions.	Answer literal questions about a *Textbook* selection.	1-120

IDENTIFYING LITERAL CAUSES AND EFFECTS

Behavioral objective	The student is asked to	Lessons
After reading a selection, the student is able to identify literal causes and effects within the selection.	Answer questions about a *Textbook* selection by identifying causes and effects.	*1-120*

RECALLING DETAILS AND EVENTS

Behavioral objective	The student is asked to	Lessons
After reading a selection, the student is able to recall details and events from the selection.	Answer questions about a *Textbook* selection by recalling details and events.	1-120

FOLLOWING WRITTEN DIRECTIONS

Behavioral objective	The student is asked to	Lessons
When presented with written directions, the student is able to follow the directions.	Complete skill exercises by following written directions.	1-120

SEQUENCING NARRATIVE EVENTS

Behavioral objective	The student is asked to	Lessons
After reading a story, the student is able to put events from the story in correct order.	Put a list of events from a *Textbook* story in correct order.	*1-120*

COMPREHENSION SKILLS: INTERPRETIVE COMPREHENSION

PREDICTING NARRATIVE OUTCOMES

Behavioral objective	The student is asked to	Lessons
While reading a story, the student is able to predict a possible story outcome.	Predict the outcome of a *Textbook* story.	*1-120*

INFERRING CAUSES AND EFFECTS

Behavioral objective	The student is asked to	Lessons
After reading a selection, the student is able to infer causes and effects within the selection.	Answer questions about a *Textbook* selection by inferring causes and effects.	*1-120*

INFERRING STORY DETAILS AND EVENTS

Behavioral objective	The student is asked to	Lessons
After reading a selection, the student is able to infer details and events within the selection.	Answer questions about a *Textbook* selection by inferring details and events.	*1-120*

MAKING COMPARISONS

Behavioral objective	The student is asked to	Lessons
When presented with a variety of sources, the student is able to make comparisons based on the sources.	Answer questions by making comparisons.	*1-120*

INFERRING MAIN IDEA

Behavioral objective	The student is asked to	Lessons
When presented with a paragraph, the student is able to infer the main idea of the paragraph.	Complete skill exercises by inferring the main idea of a specific paragraph.	15-20, 23, 24, 27, 28, 32, 35, 41, 49, 64

INFERRING DETAILS RELEVANT TO MAIN IDEA

Behavioral objective	The student is asked to	Lessons
When presented with a paragraph and its main idea, the student is able to infer details relevant to the main idea.	Complete skill exercises by inferring the details relevant to a specific main idea.	15-28, 30, 31, 34, 38, 46, 58, 69

OUTLINING

Behavioral objective	The student is asked to	Lessons
When presented with a passage containing two or more paragraphs, the student is able to outline the passage by specifying the main ideas and their supporting details.	Complete skill exercises by outlining the main ideas and supporting details of a specific passage.	80-84, 116, 120

COMPREHENSION SKILLS: REASONING

DRAWING CONCLUSIONS

Behavioral objective	The student is asked to	Lessons
After reading a selection, the student is able to draw conclusions based on evidence from the selection.	Answer questions about a *Textbook* selection by drawing conclusions.	*1-120*

EVALUATING PROBLEMS AND SOLUTIONS

Behavioral objective	The student is asked to	Lessons
After reading a selection, the student is able to evaluate problems and solutions within the selection.	Answer questions about a *Textbook* selection by evaluating problems and solutions.	*1-120*

DISTINGUISHING BETWEEN RELEVANT AND IRRELEVANT EVIDENCE

Behavioral objective	The student is asked to	Lessons
When presented with facts and evidence, the student is able to determine which evidence is relevant to each fact and which evidence is irrelevant.	Complete skill exercises by determining whether given evidence is relevant or irrelevant to given facts.	21-31, 33, 37, 42, 47, 61, 74

IDENTIFYING CONTRADICTIONS

Behavioral objective	The student is asked to	Lessons
When presented with a text containing contradictory sentences, the student is able to identify the contradictory sentences.	1) Explain how a given statement contradicts a given fact.	32-34
	2) Identify sentences within a text that contradict a given fact and then explain the contradiction.	35, 36
	3) Identify contradictory sentences within a text and then explain the contradiction.	37-42, 45, 65, 72, 85, 106

COMPLETING WRITTEN DEDUCTIONS

Behavioral objective	The student is asked to	Lessons
When presented with the major and minor premises of a formal written deduction, the student is able to complete the deduction by drawing a conclusion.	Write the conclusion for a formal written deduction.	54-59, 61-64, 97

DISTINGUISHING BETWEEN LITERAL AND INFERENTIAL QUESTIONS

Behavioral objective	The student is asked to	Lessons
When presented with a group of questions about a text, the student is able to distinguish between the literal questions and the inferential questions.	Answer questions about a text and then indicate whether the answers came from specific words in the text (literal) or from inference (inferential).	56-60, 63, 66, 68, 71, 76, 86, 102, 113

IDENTIFYING LOGICAL FALLACIES

Behavioral objective	The student is asked to	Lessons
When presented with a text containing a logical fallacy, the student is able to identify and explain the fallacy.	1) Learn seven rules for identifying logical fallacies, such as "Just because you know about a part doesn't mean you know about the whole thing."	94-120
	2) Complete skill exercises by explaining how a given text breaks one of the rules.	94-120
	3) Complete skill exercises by identifying which rule a given text breaks.	110-120

LITERARY SKILLS: ANALYZING CHARACTERS AND SETTINGS

INTERPRETING A CHARACTER'S FEELINGS

Behavioral objective	The student is asked to	Lessons
After reading a story, the student is able to interpret the feelings of a story character.	Answer questions about a *Textbook* story by interpreting a character's feelings.	*1-120*

PRETENDING TO BE A CHARACTER

Behavioral objective	The student is asked to	Lessons
After reading a story, the student is able to play the role of a story character.	Answer questions about a *Textbook* story by pretending to be a story character.	*1-120*

INTERPRETING A CHARACTER'S MOTIVES

Behavioral objective	The student is asked to	Lessons
After reading a story, the student is able to interpret the motives of a story character.	Answer questions about a *Textbook* story by interpreting a character's motives.	*1-120*

INFERRING A CHARACTER'S POINT OF VIEW

Behavioral objective	The student is asked to	Lessons
After reading a story, the student is able to infer the point of view of a story character.	Answer questions about a *Textbook* story by inferring a character's point of view.	*1-120*

PREDICTING A CHARACTER'S ACTIONS

Behavioral objective	The student is asked to	Lessons
While reading a story, the student is able to predict the actions of a story character.	Answer questions about a *Textbook* story by predicting a character's actions.	*1-120*

IDENTIFYING FEATURES OF A SETTING

Behavioral objective	The student is asked to	Lessons
After reading a story, the student is able to identify the important features of each story setting.	Complete skill exercises by matching settings with their features.	*1-120*

IDENTIFYING A CHARACTER'S TRAITS

Behavioral objective	The student is asked to	Lessons
After reading a story, the student is able to identify the important traits of each story character.	Complete skill exercises by matching characters with their traits.	*1-120*

LITERARY SKILLS: LITERARY DEVICES

INTERPRETING SIMILES

Behavioral objective	The student is asked to	Lessons
When presented with a simile, the student is able to explain what the simile means.	1) Identify which two things a given simile compares and then explain how those things are the same.	39-44, 46, 53, 62, 72, 84
	2) Transform literal statements into similes.	47-50, 70, 78, 96
	3) Identify similes within a given text.	57-60

INTERPRETING EXAGGERATION

Behavioral objective	The student is asked to	Lessons
When presented with an exaggeration, the student is able to explain what the exaggeration means.	1) Identify which part of a given exaggeration stretches the truth.	45-48, 55, 69, 88, 108
	2) Rewrite a given exaggeration so that it does not stretch the truth.	45-48, 55, 69, 88, 108
	3) Identify the exaggerations within a given text.	57-60

INTERPRETING METAPHORS

Behavioral objective	The student is asked to	Lessons
When presented with a metaphor, the student is able to explain what the metaphor means.	1) Identify which two things a given metaphor compares and then explain how those two things are the same.	49-56, 67, 77, 107
	2) Identify metaphors within a given text.	57-60

INTERPRETING SARCASM

Behavioral objective	The student is asked to	Lessons
When presented with sarcasm, the student is able to explain what the sarcasm means.	Identify sarcastic statements within a given text and use evidence from the text to explain what the sarcasm means.	59-62, 71, 88

INTERPRETING EXTENDED DIALOGUES

Behavioral objective	The student is asked to	Lessons
When presented with a lengthy dialogue in which the speakers are not always identified, the student is able to identify who says what.	1) Read descriptions of several characters and then identify which character might make a given statement.	61-64
	2) Identify the unnamed speaker for each line of an extended dialogue.	65-67, 79, 110

INTERPRETING SUBSTITUTE WORDS

Behavioral objective	The student is asked to	Lessons
When presented with a sentence containing pronouns or other referents, the student is able to explain the meaning of each pronoun or referent.	1) Read individual sentences with substitute words and identify the person or thing to which each substitute word refers.	66-68
	2) Read paragraphs with substitute words and identify the person or thing to which each substitute word refers.	71-75, 101

INTERPRETING SHORTENED SENTENCES

Behavioral objective	The student is asked to	Lessons
When presented with a sentence that omits words, the student is able to identify the omitted words.	Identify which words have been omitted from a given sentence and then insert those words into the sentence.	69-73, 89

INTERPRETING COMBINED SENTENCES

Behavioral objective	The student is asked to	Lessons
When presented with a sentence containing an appositive, the student is able to recognize the appositive and explain its meaning.	1) Form a single sentence containing an appositive by combining two sentences.	74-78, 83, 104
	2) Form two sentences from a single sentence containing an appositive.	76-78, 86
	3) Insert an appositive into a given sentence.	79-83, 91

INTERPRETING IRONY

Behavioral objective	The student is asked to	Lessons
After reading a story, the student is able to identify and explain ironic situations in the story.	1) Recognize that literary irony occurs when a character acts on the basis of a mistaken belief.	88-90
	2) Explain given examples of literary irony.	88-92, 96, 102, 111

LITERARY SKILLS: TYPES OF LITERATURE

READING DIFFERENT TYPES OF LITERATURE

Behavioral objective	The student is asked to	Lessons
When presented with different types of literature, the student is able to read them.	Read the following types of literature in the *Textbook*:	
	– fantasy	5-13, 29-34, 73-75
	– short stories	1-3, 14-34, 50-57, 73-75
	– novels	5-13, 36-49, 59-70 91-120
	– biographies	76-82
	– poetry	35, 36, 58, 59 71-73, 86, 87
	– plays	83-85

STUDY SKILLS: WRITING

WRITING ANSWERS TO QUESTIONS

Behavioral objective	The student is asked to	Lessons
When presented with a written question, the student is able to write the correct answer.	Write the answers to questions presented in the *Skillbook* and *Workbook*.	1-120

COMPLETING WRITING ASSIGNMENTS

Behavioral objective	The student is asked to	Lessons
When presented with a specific writing assignment, the student is able to complete the assignment by writing a complete paragraph.	Complete writing assignments presented in the *Skillbook*.	1-120

STUDY SKILLS: USING REFERENCE MATERIALS

READING INFORMATIONAL PASSAGES

Behavioral objective	The student is asked to	Lessons
When presented with an informational passage, the student is able to read it.	Read informational passages in the *Textbook*.	1, 4, 21, 24, 27, 36, 56, 60, 71, 73, 76, 87-90, 92, 97, 106, 113

INTERPRETING MAPS

Behavioral objective	The student is asked to	Lessons
When presented with a map, the student is able to interpret it correctly.	1) Use a given map to answer questions about direction, relative size, proximity, labels, and other map-related concepts.	4-13, 15, 17, 18, 21, 23, 24, 27, 33, 40, 63, 67, 68, 70, 71, 73-76, 78-80, 83, 85, 87-90, 102
	2) Use a given map to determine whether statements are true or false.	91-93, 98, 99, 109

FILLING OUT FORMS

Behavioral objective	The student is asked to	Lessons
When presented with a blank standard form, the student is able to fill it out correctly.	Complete skill exercises by filling out standard forms.	81-84, 87, 103, 114

IDENTIFYING PROPER REFERENCE SOURCES

Behavioral objective	The student is asked to	Lessons
When presented with the need for a reference source, the student is able to identify which reference source to consult.	Identify the appropriate use of atlases, dictionaries, and encyclopedias.	85-90, 94

INTERPRETING GRAPHS

Behavioral objective	The student is asked to	Lessons
When presented with a graph, the student is able to interpret it correctly.	1) Use a given graph to answer questions about quantity, change, and other graph-related concepts.	92-97
	2) Use a given graph to determine whether statements are true or false.	100, 101, 105, 115

Skills Profile Folder

Name: ______________________

The following chart may be reproduced to make a skills profile folder for each student. The chart summarizes the skills presented in *Reading Mastery VI* and provides space for indicating when a student has mastered each skill.

	SKILL	LESSON RANGE	DATE MASTERED
DECODING SKILLS	**WORDS**		
	Regularly Spelled Words Orally reads lists of regularly spelled words	1-120	
	Irregularly Spelled Words Orally reads lists of irregularly spelled words	1-120	
	SENTENCES AND STORIES		
	Oral Reading Reads text orally	1-120	
	Silent Reading Reads story silently	1-120	
COMPREHENSION SKILLS	**COMPREHENSION READINESS**		
	Following Directions Follows directions presented orally by teacher	1-120	
	VOCABULARY		
	Common Words and Phrases Explains meanings of common words and phrases used in text	1-120	
	Vocabulary Definitions Comprehends written definitions of vocabulary words	1-120	
	Using Words in Context Uses vocabulary words in sentences	1-120	
	Crossword Puzzles Uses vocabulary words to complete crossword puzzle	21-91	

	SKILL	LESSON RANGE	DATE MASTERED
COMPREHENSION SKILLS	**Word Meaning from Context** Uses sentence context to predict meaning of vocabulary word	3-120	
	LITERAL COMPREHENSION		
	Literal Questions Answers literal questions about text	1-120	
	Cause and Effect Identifies literal causes and effects in text	1-120	
	Details and Events Recalls text details and events	1-120	
	Following Directions Follows written directions	1-120	
	Sequencing Puts text events in order	1-120	
	INTERPRETIVE COMPREHENSION		
	Predicting Outcomes Predicts outcome of story	1-120	
	Causes and Effects Infers causes and effects in text	1-120	
	Inferring Details and Events Infers details and events in text	1-120	
	Comparisons Makes comparisons based on variety of sources	1-120	
	Main Idea Infers main idea of specific paragraphs	15-64	

(continued on page 77)

Skills Profile Folder - page 2

Name: ____________________

	SKILL	LESSON RANGE	DATE MASTERED
COMPREHENSION SKILLS	**Relevant Details** Infers details relevant to specific main idea	15-69	
	Outlining Outlines main ideas and supporting details of specific passage	80-120	
	REASONING		
	Drawing Conclusions Draws conclusions based on text	1-120	
	Problems and Solutions Evaluates problems and solutions	1-120	
	Relevant and Irrelevant Evidence Determines whether given evidence is relevant or irrelevant to given facts	21-74	
	Contradictions Explains how a given statement contradicts a given fact	32-34	
	Identifies sentences that contradict a given fact and explains contradiction	35-36	
	Identifies contradictory sentences and explains contradiction	37-106	
	Deductions Writes conclusions for formal written deductions	54-97	
	Literal and Inferential Questions Distinguishes between literal and inferential questions	56-113	

	SKILL	LESSON RANGE	DATE MASTERED
COMP SKILLS	**Fallacies** Learns seven rules for identifying fallacies	94-120	
	Explains how given text breaks one of the rules	94-120	
	Identifies rule that given text breaks	110-120	
LITERARY SKILLS	**ANALYZING CHARACTERS AND SETTINGS**		
	Feelings Interprets feelings of story character	1-120	
	Role Playing Pretends to be story character	1-120	
	Motives Interprets motives of story character	1-120	
	Point of View Infers point of view of story character	1-120	
	Prediction Predicts actions of story character	1-120	
	Settings Identifies features of story settings	1-120	
	Traits Identifies traits of story characters	1-120	
	LITERARY DEVICES		
	Similes Explains meaning of given simile	39-84	
	Changes literal statement into simile	47-96	
	Identifies similes within text	57-60	

(continued on page 78)

Skills Profile Folder - page 3

Name: ____________________

Category	SKILL	LESSON RANGE	DATE MASTERED
LITERARY SKILLS	**Exaggeration** Identifies how exaggeration stretches truth	45-108	
	Rewrites exaggeration so it no longer exaggerates	45-108	
	Identifies exaggeration within text	57-60	
	Metaphors Explains meaning of given metaphor	49-107	
	Identifies metaphors within text	57-60	
	Sarcasm Interprets sarcasm	59-88	
	Extended Dialogues Interprets extended dialogues by identifying unnamed speakers	61-110	
	Substitute Words Interprets sentences that use pronouns and other substitute words	66-101	
	Shortened Sentences Interprets sentences that omit words	69-89	
	Combined Sentences Combines two sentences by using appositive	74-104	
	Changes sentence containing appositive into two sentences	76-86	
	Inserts appositive into sentence	79-91	
	Irony Recognizes and interprets literary irony	88-111	

Category	SKILL	LESSON RANGE	DATE MASTERED
LITERARY SKILLS	**TYPES OF LITERATURE**		
	Realistic Fiction Reads realistic fiction	1-120	
	Fantasy Reads fantasy	5-75	
	Short Stories Reads short stories	1-75	
	Novels Reads complete novels	5-120	
	Biographies Reads biography	76-82	
	Poetry Reads poems	35-87	
	Drama Reads play	83-85	
STUDY SKILLS	**WRITING**		
	Answering Questions Writes answers to written questions	1-120	
	Writing Assignments Completes daily writing assignments	1-120	
	USING REFERENCE MATERIALS		
	Informational Passages Reads informational passages	1-113	
	Maps Interprets maps	4-109	
	Forms Fills out standard forms	81-114	
	Reference Sources Identifies appropriate use of atlases, dictionaries, and encyclopedias	85-94	
	Graphs Interprets graphs	92-115	